MY DELUSIONAL WORLD

SAJIT ABRAHAM

Rushmore Press LLC
www.rushmorepress.com
1 888 733 9607

ISBN Softcover 978-1-950818-06-8

Printed in the United States of America.

Table of Contents

Chapter 1

A SMALL JAIL CELL

My name is Gaddy Das.

I am 28 years old.

I am sitting in a jail cell in Hamilton, Alabama.

I was born in Canada but come from an Indian background. I am currently living in the United States.

I have been arrested for indecent exposure. I hear voices echoing all around me. They tell me that once I get out of jail, I will become a famous rock musician.

The bars enclose me, making me feel like a monkey in a cage. Though I am trapped here, I know good things are about to happen. The voices keep reassuring me that if I keep taking risks, I will become one of the most famous celebrities in the world.

I took a lot of risks before I was arrested. I drove my car very fast down a highway. I jumped into the shallow end of a pool, without being injured. And I went into a gas station and took my clothes off, which led to my arrest.

They give me some meals while I am in jail. The food is not great. But I am not worried. The Higher Power reassures me that things will get way better once I get out of jail.

My parents, Lillian and David Das, who are both 60-year-old, and are immigrants from India, are on vacation. I live in the same house as they do in Winfield, Alabama. I also have a sister, named Debra George, who is two years younger than me and lives in Toronto.

Before I went to jail, I bought a guitar at a music store in Winfield. I played the guitar and recorded myself on a tape recorder. The voices kept telling me that if I played guitar, I would become the most famous rock musician in the world — even better than the Beatles.

One day, while I was playing, I decided I wanted to be like the rock group "The Who" who were noted for smashing their instruments on stage. I picked up my guitar and smashed the bottom of it, breaking my guitar.

I then began playing the guitar again, feeling like I was the greatest rock musician who ever lived.

One day, while my parents were home, I asked my mother if she would listen to the rock music I had created. She listened and said it sounded really weird.

I told her that the music was very experimental, like the Beatles, and that I would soon become the greatest rock musician ever.

"Are you sure you are okay?" she asked.

"I'm fine Mum," I said, smiling at her to reassure her that everything was okay.

I hope to be released from jail soon.

Chapter 2

THE BULLY

I remember sitting in class in elementary school in Prince George.

I am in Grade 5.

I stare at the chalkboard as my teacher teaches me multiplication. My teacher is a short, stout man with a mustache. He is a kind teacher, and I enjoy being his student.

I am a good student. I study every day and always complete my homework assignments.

I am what you would call a nerd. I have a handsome complexion, but I am quite short and skinny.

The class bully always picks on me.

His name is Runyon. Runyon has failed a grade and is tougher than all the students in his class. He has several students he targets, and I am among his favorites. The other boys in the class, who are his friends, follow Runyon's lead and pick on other students in the class.

Runyon wears a jacket with a hockey logo on it. He is very good at sports. It's odd, but in school, you get way more admiration if you are good at sports but bad at academics.

Runyon is a classic example of this. I dread going outside for recess.

I know Runyon will be out there. He will be looking to target whomever he can. I try to hide from Runyon.

I decide to hang around the main entrance of the school. I figure Runyon might be elsewhere. Suddenly, I see Runyon coming towards me. He has that smile on his face,

which petrifies me.

"Hey Hindu," he says, "how's it going?"

I stare at him not being able to utter a word. "You're such a nerd," he says.

Since I am quite young, I don't shower as regularly as I should either, and I have a little bit of dandruff in my hair.

"You got lice still," he says smiling at me.

I stay still. I figure if I run, he will come after me. Suddenly, I see a teacher approaching.

He is a short, stocky teacher who teaches Grade 4. His name is Roy Jackson. As he approaches, the bully decides to walk away and not bother me anymore. Mr. Jackson approaches me and then walks right by me.

The bully has left.

It's cold outside, and I can't wait to get back indoors again.

Reading is the next subject of the day. I love reading. I read all sorts of kids' books, including those written by Don Sobol, who wrote Encyclopedia Brown. I admire Encyclopedia Brown.

He is called this because he reads encyclopedias. He is a child detective and solves mysteries. I want to be admired as he is. I want to be smart, but I would like to be admired for being smart, rather than being called a nerd all the time.

Today, we are reading some stories about Indigenous people. The stories describe cold winters and how Indigenous people live their lives. I feel warmth and comfort as I read these stories.

The only subject I find difficult in school is gym class.

I am shorter and skinnier than most of the boys in my class. I love watching sports on television, and I wish I could be as athletic as the athletes I see. I really enjoy watching football, especially the Canadian Football League and the National Football league.

I also watch hockey.

I love watching the Edmonton Oilers in the 1980s, especially watching Wayne Gretzky.

He is so amazing. He flows across the ice and shoots from difficult angles. I believe that he is not only athletic, but he also has the mind to play hockey.

I read about the history of hockey as well.

I read about Bobby Orr, and I occasionally see some stuff on television about him. When I am downstairs in the television room in our family's house, I pick up a hockey stick which my parents bought me, as well as using a tennis ball.

I pretend to be Bobby Orr.

I love sports so much. I wish I could be a better athlete. But that's the way things go, I guess.

Chapter 3

MY MOTHER'S COOKING

I remember me and my family living in a big house in Prince George.

I can smell chicken curry coming from the kitchen. My mum is such an amazing cook. Not only does she make Indian dishes, but she also makes pasta and burritos, two things I greatly enjoy.

When I am home on the weekends, I really enjoy my life. School is a tough thing to go through, especially with Runyon being around. I try to imagine every day as being a day on the weekend.

My mother is such a nice woman. She is short in stature and is so easy to be around. She admires the simple things in life, like the birds flying outside or the cold of winter or the high heat in the summer.

My family sits together for dinner every evening. We talk about our lives. I love spending time with my family.

My dad is a surgeon. He is about five feet six inches tall, is bald, and has a mustache.

He wants me to grow up to be a doctor just like him. My dad's two brothers are doctors as well.

I am doing well in school, so I figure I may end up being a doctor. My parents buy me a children's book about the human body. I read it, not completely understanding it, but very curious about what it is about.

Most of my reading is spent with sportsbooks, and children's mysteries. I really enjoy the history of sports. I love reading about the great Brazilian soccer player Pele as well as reading about Bobby Orr, the hockey player Maurice Rocket Richard, and the great C. F. L. quarterback Ron Lancaster.

Even though the winter is very cold, I really enjoy winter. The snow falls outside, and it is so peaceful. I like playing in the snow as well.

A kid living next door to me is my closest friend. He is a handsome looking kid, and I really enjoy hanging out with him. He has curly hair, and straight, white teeth.

We play outside in the winter.

We make snow forts on his front lawn. We like to hide in the snow forts. The snow fort has all sorts of short tunnels, which we try to create. We play indoors as well. We love to play with action figures and stuffed animals.

I pretend that one of my stuffed animals is like the detective Sherlock Holmes. I read Sherlock Holmes, not completely understanding all of it, since I am so young, but just admiring Holmes for being such an amazing intellectual.

My friend, whose name is Jack, admires television heroes much more. He loves Magnum P. I., and the Knight Rider.

We seem to be born of different worlds. When we play together, my stuffed animal, who is like Holmes, and his stuffed animal, who is like Magnum P.I., get together and solve mysteries and hunt down the bad guys.

Besides playing with stuffed animals, we also create short stories together. I do the writing while he creates illustrations. We really have fun doing this together. He also enjoys creating model airplanes, which he hangs all over his room.

I also play the violin and the piano.

I go for lessons every week. I practice every day. Even though I am pretty good, I am not the best violinist there. There are two young Chinese Canadian brothers, I know, who are absolutely amazing.

I want to be as good as them, but I don't have their work ethic when I am young. They practice way more than I do. We compete in a music festival every year in Prince George, and they win all the awards.

They are also very good at academics. Even though I am good at school, I feel envious of them because they work much harder than I do.

When I come home from school, I do my homework, and then I watch a lot of television. I watch shows like Happy Days and Three's Company. If I want to be the greatest violinist, or student, I need to work harder.

The other problem is that most of the kids in my class are more into trying to be cool rather than being smart. I am made fun of because I want to be smart. The kids at school are more worried about which 80's rock bands are the greatest, or how cool they dress or how good at sports they are.

Deep down, I want to be cool as well.

But my parents, and the kids whom I play the violin with, encourage me to be into more intellectual things.

I dream about wanting to become muscular. I want to be able to fight the bully and win the hearts of the girls in my class. Though I am still quite young, eight years old, I still dream of gaining the respect of girls.

In school, we do square dancing.

Most of the girls in my class don't want to dance with me because I am not considered good looking.

I sit in my room and dream of being athletic and muscular.

Chapter 4

THE DRAWING

I remember being 13 years old.

I am sitting at a desk in my room in Prince George constructing a drawing for my drafting class. There is a lamp on my desk, which emits a big, blue light.

I am terrible at drawing. My drawing looks disjointed. I marvel at those who can draw very well like Jack. Jack moved away to Victoria, and even though its been a few years since I saw him, I still miss him being here.

I have no close friends now.

I lone most of the time. However, I also enjoy being by myself.

As I sit and draw, I hope the teacher doesn't give me a really bad mark on my drawing. I spend some time on it, and then I go and watch television. The Cosby Show is on, and it's one of my favorite shows.

I enjoy the show because it isn't too serious. My mood lightens up every time I watch the show.

Suddenly, it's dinnertime.

I sit with my family at the kitchen table. I start to tell my parents about how awful my drafting class is.

"My drawing looks terrible," I say.

"Don't give up," says my father. "Keep working on it."

The next day, I go to school. Drafting class is in the afternoon.

We are asked to work on our homework assignments in class.

I feel very insecure about my drawing, and am wishing that the teacher had not asked us to work on our drawings in class.

Runyon is in my drafting class.

The teacher leaves the classroom for a bit. Runyon approaches me.

"Hey nerd, what is that supposed to be?" he says. "Ah nothing," I say.

Suddenly, Runyon grabs my drawing. He starts parading it all over the class. A friend of Runyon's, named Jason, a tall stocky kid, sees my drawing and starts laughing.

"Hey nerd," he says, "what is that supposed to be?"

Suddenly, the teacher comes back. He is a short, skinny man with an older looking complexion. However, by that time, Runyon has already returned to his desk.

I want to tell the teacher what happened, but I am too afraid to because of what Runyon might do to me. Also, telling on people is not something that you do in high school.

I have told my parents once about Runyon, but if I tell them again, and they get concerned, they may come to the school and confront Runyon. This would be something, which I don't want to happen.

Runyon also has a girlfriend.

And the girls at school seem to like him. I feel miserable. Again, we do square dancing in gym period, and the girls don't want to dance with me. Some of them stand beside me, and they won't even hold my hand.

I try to figure out why girls like Runyon and not me. Runyon is mean. Do girls like guys who are mean to them? It makes absolutely no sense. He is also as dumb as an ox.

Do women like unintelligent guys?

However, he is also athletic, which might explain why they are attracted to him.

Besides myself, there are three other boys I hang out with, who are considered to be nerds as well. One of the boys is named George. George wears glasses, and looks quite nerdy. He is very good at math and playing chess.

I play chess as well. Sometimes, we play together at lunchtime. I love chess because I find it very relaxing.

When we are in gym, during square dancing, George and I end up sitting out of most of the dances because the girls don't want to dance with us. George has a bit more of a sense of humor about this than I do.

"Oh well," he says, "that's just the way it goes."

I say nothing in response. It' s all just too embarrassing.

Chapter 5

VOICES

It is at age 13 that I start hearing voices.

The voices mock me, telling me I am a nerd, and that I am too scrawny.

I lie on my bed, listening to the voices. I want to tell people what I am going through, but I don't think anybody will believe me. They might think I am making up some kind of story in order to get sympathy.

The voices are bothersome, but I am still able to cope. I hear the voices most clearly when I am by myself, but they are also there when I am around other people. They are distracting, but not so distracting that I can't cope with them.

The voices sound similar to the taunts from Runyon and his friends. Perhaps, they have caused me to hear voices like this. I can't say for sure. I wonder if others who have been teased by Runyon hear voices like mine.

Back at school, me and some friends, my nerdy friends, are discussing rock music.

We all agree that the best bands existed during the 1960s. One of the other nerdy friends, who is named Guy, who is stocky and pimply-faced, says that his favorite rock band is Creedence Clearwater Revival.

"They rule," says Guy.

"The music nowadays sucks," says George. "I can' t stand Michael Jackson and Prince and Madonna. Their music sounds so superficial."

"The Beatles are the greatest too," says Guy. "I agree," I say.

However, despite my saying that to my nerdy friends, when it comes to discussing this topic with others in the school, I remain a closeted admirer of the 1960's rock music.

I really believe that it is the best music, but others will criticize me even more if I dare tell them.

One day, Runyon asks me this question.

"Hey, who's your favorite band nerd?" he asks.

Ah, I like either Motley Crue or R. A. T. T.," I say.

Runyon stares at me quizzically.

"Are you bullshitting me?" asks Runyon.

"No, I don' think so," hoping the idiot will go away.

Other friends of Runyon's ask George who his favorite band is.

"The Monkees, The Beatles, CCR," says George.

"They suck," says one of Runyon's friends. "They don't suck at all," says George. "Compared to the music nowadays, they totally rule."

Despite being called uncool, for the most part, I admire George for not being afraid to say what he feels. I am not quite this way.

One of the Chinese Canadian brothers who plays the violin is emphatic that he is only a classical music listener. He constantly talks about Mozart and Beethoven. I even heard that he carried a ghetto blaster around school, playing classical music on it to defy others who paraded a ghetto blaster around school with only rock music on it.

"That music is so loud and obnoxious," he says.

"I can't even understand what they are singing about."

At home, I listen to the Beatles all the time. I marvel at songs like 'I am the Walrus," 'Hey Jude," and 'Let it Be." They were so creative; I think to myself. No one else can create music like that.

Despite all of that though, I still think about my inner conflict, wanting to be a cool kid and yet enjoying nerdy things. I still have dreams about being a muscular kid, and being very good looking to women.

The voices don' t help either.

I don't want to be called scrawny and nerdy. I wish I was more into Motley Crue.

But I really can't enjoy Motley Crue. It is so superficial, and the music is just a lot of noise, rather than being poetic and beautiful.

I guess life is just like this, and there isn't anything I can do about it.

Chapter 6

NEWHIGHSCHOOL

I am now 15 years old.

And I have moved to a new high school in Prince George.

I am doing an advanced, academic program at the new school called the International Baccalaureate Program. I feel happy to have left my old high school. No more days worrying about being picked on by Runyon.

I do worry, however, about what the new school will be like.

Will there be another Runyon to deal with?

The school is much bigger as well.

The first day of classes seems very demanding. Math class is especially very difficult. Before I coasted through most of my courses, but now things seem too challenging.

The first day I meet a kid named Doug. We decide to share a locker. Doug is a tall, skinny kid who really loves sports. We talk about sports quite a bit, as well as discussing how difficult our courses are.

"Yeah," says Doug. "It's way harder. I hope I survive this year." "I know," I say. "Life has become much more difficult for sure." A few days later, I meet a kid named Tim. Tim is Vietnamese Canadian. Tim and I hit it off really well, and we end up becoming best friends.

We sit together in all our classes.

Tim also finds the program very challenging.

Our teacher for math, who is also in charge of the Baccalaureate program, is a skinny woman with greyish hair. She is strict, and most of us find it difficult to follow her.

"I don't know what the hell is going on in that class," says Tim. "I know," I say.

She also gives us a lot of homework.

Before I could get good grades and watch a lot of television at the same time. Now it is much different.

There is another kid in the program named James.

James is a cool looking kid with a punk hairdo. He is the true definition of a rebel. Not only is he very smart, but also, he is very attractive to women.

I admire James and wish I could be more like him. He skips classes a lot, and he ends up arguing with all our teachers, especially the math teacher. Everybody thinks he is so cool.

I decide to change my appearance a little because of James. I start wearing mousse in my hair. James also rolls his pants up like they do on the show Miami Vice. I do the same thing, and start to feel more attractive.

Women seem to like me more.

The other thing, which I am good at, which seems to impress women, is my ability to do impressions of famous celebrities.

I give a presentation in math class, where I do impressions of famous politicians and Hollywood celebrities. Everybody laughs at my humor, and they seem to find me to be the comedic type.

I have never felt so good in my entire life. I am now considered cooler than I was before.

However, I still have problems with my body image. I am very skinny.

My parents buy a rowing machine. I use the machine a lot, but I don't end up getting any bigger or any more muscular. What I need is weights — but I am too afraid to go to the gym.

Tim, who despite being attractive, feels the same way about himself. We talk about the women in our class, and how we would like to be their boyfriend.

"Man, we're such losers," says Tim.

"We're not that bad," I say.

"Then why aren't we going out with women?" asks Tim. "I don't know," I say.

The other thing we have in common is that we are both Asian Canadian and our parents don't encourage us to date.

"They just don't get it," says Tim. "They don't understand what it's like growing up here. It's totally different where they came from."

We both admire James, his cool persona and his ability to attract women.

"I wish I was more like James," I say to Tim.

"Me too," says Tim. "If only we could be more like that."

Chapter 7

THE POEM

Tim and I are wandering down the halls of the high school, when we pass a girl in the hallway. She is Indo-Canadian and very pretty. She has curly hair and beautiful brown eyes. She is wearing jeans and a sweatshirt.

She is putting stuff into her locker.

Suddenly, she stares at me for a bit, and then smiles a little. We walk past her.

"Who's that?" I ask Tim. Tim smiles at me.

"Her name is Sally."

"Sally. Man, she is really hot."

"I think she likes you," says Tim with a grin. "You think so?"

"Yeah, you big stud."

Tim laughs and I smile as well. All I can think is how far I have come since my days of dealing with women who wouldn't even hold hands with me when dancing.

"You should ask her out," says Tim. "Yeah, I wish I could do that," I say.

Suddenly, I pause and a thought dawns on me.

"I know what I can do," I say with glee. "Maybe I can write some kind of a poem for her, and leave it in her locker. That's really original, and I know girls really like that kind of thing,"

"Go for it," says Tim. "You've got nothing to lose." Later, I arrive home.

There is a book of poetry my parents bought a long time ago. I decide to look through the book and see what kind of poetry I can find. There are poems by all sorts of famous writers like William Shakespeare, Percy Shelley, William Wordsworth, Samuel Coleridge.

I find a poem by Lord Byron.

The poem is called 'She Walks in Beauty.'

> "She walks in beauty like the night of cloudless climes and starry skies. And all that's best of dark and bright Meet in her aspect and her eyes; thus, mellowed to that tender light which heaven to gaudy day denies.
> One shade the more, one ray the less Had half impaired the nameless grace, which waves in every raven tress, or softly lightens o'er her face; Where thoughts serene sweet express
> How pure, how dear their dwelling place.
>
> And on that cheek, and o'er that brow, So soft, so calm, and yet eloquent,
> The smiles that win the tints of that glow, But full of days in goodness spent
> A mind at peace with all below A heart whose love is innocent."
>
> I read over the poem, happy as I can be.
> I know she is going to like it. Finally, my first girlfriend is all I can think.
> The next day I see Tim in math class. "Did you do it?" he asks, smiling.

"Not yet. I'll do it after math class. I just have to make sure she doesn't see me slip it into her locker. The poem is amazing," I say. "It's a poem by Lord Byron, really romantic and full of all kinds of things that women really want to hear."

Math class is slowly ticking to an end. It seems like math class, more than usual, is taking forever.

Finally, class is over.

"Tim, will you come with me?" I ask. "Yeah, no problem," says Tim.

We approach Sally's locker. She is not there.

I slip the poem into the locker. I feel nervous and sweaty. I can only dream of what she'll say when she sees it. My heart starts to skip beats.

The next day Tim and I see Sally walking down the hallway with a friend.

Nervously, I call out to Sally, asking if she has seen my poem. Her friend replies.

"She thought it was really sweet. But she has a boyfriend already."

"God damn, I whisper. "Sorry about that," I say.

"It's okay," says her friend smiling at me.

Despite it not working out, I still feel good. At least she liked me. In the end, I end up feeling like a winner. I have a cool reputation now, rather than a nerdy one, which makes me feel happier.

Chapter 8

THE DORM

I am now 18 years old and looking forward to going to university.

Tim and I are both going to the same university. We are attending the University of British Columbia in Vancouver.

I am at Tim's house.

"Man, I can't wait," says Tim, rubbing his hands together. "I know," I say.

"No more parents to worry about. And all the women down there — it'll be so awesome,"

A few days later, I arrive in Vancouver.

I am going to stay at one of the dorms on campus. Even though I really wanted to room with Tim, I decide not to because I am afraid, I won't get any studying done. Instead, I room with a guy named Bob.

Bob is very smart, and very nerdy. He is also in the Baccalaureate program. He is tall and skinny and wears glasses. He is a great chess player. Sometimes, we play chess and he always ends up beating me. The nerdish part of me really likes Bob, while the cool part prefers Tim.

My parents help me to get everything in my dorm room organized. They then head back to Prince George. I sit on the bed in my dorm room. The space has a desk and a bed with my computer on top of my desk.

Tim comes over from the dormitory he is staying in.

He knocks on the door. Bob is somewhere else. "Man, we're free," says Tim, entering the room. "I know — I can't wait to meet the girls," I say.

A few days later, classes start. Tim and I are still trying to study as much as we can. We both really want to do well in university.

When it comes to my family, many in my family are doctors. My dad, who is a surgeon, has two brothers who are both doctors as well. My dad and mother really want me to go into medicine. My mother is also a doctor but decided not to practice.

"If you go into medicine, you can survive and have enough money to live on," says my dad. "Remember to study as hard as you can. In the end, hard work always pays off."

I decide to enroll in the genetics program at U. B. C.

I go to class every day and I pay attention. However, my courses are a lot more demanding than I thought they would be.

I take chemistry courses and math courses as well.

The chemistry courses have all sorts of weird diagrams of atoms and molecules, things which I have great difficulty understanding. We are supposed to memorize a lot of this stuff, which again I find very difficult.

The math courses are very difficult as well. I am doing Calculus.

I keep doing the same problems over and over again, trying to solve them, but I can't seem to get the answers right.

Tm and I study together at the library. We spend at least a few hours there.

Tim is having the same problems as I am.

"What the hell?" says Tim with frustration. "I didn't know our courses would end up being this difficult."

Tim also wants to become a doctor. "This is brutal," he says.

After studying, Tim and I either go and play tennis on the university courts or we go to either of our dorms and play pool.

I also meet some girls in some of my classes. However, even though I have become cooler, I am still very skinny, and I hear voices telling me that I am still kind of scrawny.

"He's really sweet," a woman's voice says to me. "But he's just not quite big enough."

I want to go to the gym and get bigger. There are gyms everywhere on campus. However, I am too afraid to go, having to stand in front of huge jocks who would totally embarrass me.

It rains a lot in Vancouver.

Tim and I start to feel a little depressed about the way things are going.

"I thought we had it made down here," he says.

Tim and I are in his dorm room, which he shares with someone else. We have ordered pizza, which is what we do when we get together during the weekend.

We discuss some of the marks we have gotten.

"I think I nearly failed every exam so far," says Tim.

"The only course that is going well for me is English," I say. "God Gaddy, what happens if we fail out?"

"I hope we don't," I say.

"God, I thought Vancouver would be so great. No more parents, lots of women around.

"In the end, we're still a bunch of losers," says Tim. "We're not losers," I say. "We just need to hang in there." "God, it rains so much here. It's depressing," says Tim. "I know," I say, "I know."

Chapter 9

GETTING DRUNK

During the weekend, the dorm is having a drinking party.

We will be drinking shooters.

I have never had more than a glass of beer in my entire life.

The cool person in me wants me to drink with the boys. The nerdier half is not particularly in love with this idea. I am still not sure what to do until the weekend arrives, when I decide I will listen to the cool half.

The reason is I have never really drunk before, and I want to know what the experience is like.

Bob is not in favor of the idea.

"I'm leaving," says Bob. "I'm not going to sit around and get drunk all weekend."

"Why not Bob?" I ask.

"It is just not a good thing to do."

"Don't you want to know what it feels like?" "No, I don't," says Bob, emphatically.

Bob leaves around five in the evening.

At about seven, the drinking begins. We are all sitting in a dorm ready to gulp down as many shooters as we possibly can. The nerdier half of me thinks this is crazy, but the cool half realizes that to be cool, you have to drink with the boys.

I start drinking one shooter. Everybody downs their shooters.

We are expected to drink as many as we can during the evening. After about the third shooter, I start to feel really drunk. "This is so cool," I say, giggling away.

"I can't believe I never did this before."

Suddenly, however, my stomach feels queasy. The other guys in the dorm tell me to take a break and go to the bathroom.

Before I reach the bathroom, I vomit heavily. My puke is all over the floor leading to the toilets. I run to a toilet, and start vomiting everything out. Suddenly, the nerdier half takes over.

I can't believe I did this the nerdier half says. I am feeling absolutely miserable.

After vomiting like crazy, I head back to my dorm room. I lay down. I have a horrible headache.

Suddenly, there is a knock on the door.

"Was it you who vomited out there?" asks a dorm mate. "Yeah," I say, groggily "it was me."

He tells me that one of the dorm mates ran into the bathroom and slipped over all the vomit on the floor.

I find out it was Hank. Hank has blond hair and blue eyes, and stands about five feet nine inches tall.

"Yeah, Hank hit the deck," the dorm mate says. "Is he okay?" I ask.

"Yeah, he fell pretty heavily, but he is fine." Later, I fall asleep.

I wake up a little as I hear the door open and shut. Bob is back.

He goes to bed.

In the morning, I wake up with a really bad headache.

I sleep in till 11 a.m., and then I have a coffee in the dorm's cafeteria.

I come back to the dorm room. Bob is there.

"What happened last night?" Bob asks. "I got drunk, Bob."

Bob seems displeased.

"What a waste of time," he says.

Bob makes me feel compassion for my nerdier side. I should not have gotten drunk, I think. This was just wasteful and not worth it.

Suddenly, as I walk down the hallway, a dorm mate, who is Chinese-Canadian and has glasses greets me.

"Hey Master Blaster, how's it going?" he says. "Master what?" I say.

"Yeah, you have a new nickname," he says. "What you did was legendary. I haven't seen many people vomit like that."

"Thanks," I say.

Just about everybody I see in the dorm now addresses me as Master Blaster.

I leave the dorm for a bit, and later come back.

When I come back, on our room door is a printed picture of a dragon vomiting his guts out.

Bob sees me.

"That's just crazy," he says.

"Oh well, live and let live," I say.

Later on, that day, I walk over to Tim's dorm. Tim tells me he did the same thing I did.

"I got really drunk and threw up too," he says laughing. "It was fun," he says.

"I guess so," I say, half-heartedly agreeing with Tim.

As for my nickname, it's something I have never really come to terms with.

Chapter 10

FAILURE

My first year of university is over.

It is summer holidays, and I am returning to Prince George to my parent's place.

I feel miserable.

I am convinced that I have failed almost every course I have taken. I tell my parents, who are disappointed with my academic performance.

Although, they don't say much, I think they feel that I haven't studied enough and that I goofed off all year.

I feel very depressed.

I am to the point of being suicidal.

Tim is my only consolation. We both fear the worst. "I don't want to see my grades," says Tim.

"Same here," I say

We see each other a lot during the summer holidays.

Most days, we go outside and play tennis, then go back to Tim's place and watch a movie.

"Have you told your parents?" I ask Tim.

"No," says Tim. "I am so afraid of them finding out how I did that I really don't want to tell them."

I spend the entire summer thinking about how I did, and what I could do to improve. I studied as hard as I could, I thought. It is just I might not be meant for sciences.

I had done well in English.

But everything else was a bowl of misery.

During the summer, I read a book by Joseph Campbell, a famous author, and mythologist. He says so many things I agree with. He believes all religions are equal, and that in this world, you should follow your bliss.

I start thinking about how to follow my bliss. I talk to Tim about it.

"I think I am not meant for sciences," I say. "The only problem is my parents might not agree with me."

"You should do what you are good at," says Tim. "I know, but how?"

A few weeks later, we receive our grades. I am so scared to open the envelope.

I open it, and stare at the grades. I'm surprised.

I barely pass every course. It is amazing. I think they passed me because they wanted my parents' money for another year.

My parents look at the grades.

"So, you get to go back," says my Mum. "Yeah," I say half smiling.

My dad says nothing.

I am relieved I get to go back. Despite having some thoughts about not going into the sciences again, I decide to do sciences again. I really want to please my parents and be a doctor.

Later on, I phone Tim.

"How did you do?" I ask Tim. Tim squirms a bit.

And then pauses. "I failed", he says.

"Oh my God, do your parents know?"

"No, I managed to hide it from them. There is no way I'm going to tell them about it. God, I feel miserable."

"I'll come over," I say.

We sit in Tim's basement watching a movie. "What are you going to do?" I ask.

"When we go back to Vancouver, I am going to enroll at a community college there," says Tim. "I'll have to lie to my parents and tell them that I am going to U. B. C."

"Are you sure you can keep that a secret?" I ask. "Yeah, I think I can. There's no other way."

Another thing I think is that my parents are spoiling me because they don't ask me to get a job during the summer.

All of the kids I know at university have summer jobs. I feel like such a loser because I am not working.

My parents are paying my way, however, so I do whatever I can to please them, including becoming a doctor.

The other thing that is bothering me a little is the voices I have been hearing.

I hear mainly women's voices. telling me that I am a sweet guy, but that I am not big enough to satisfy them.

"I can't believe how depressed I am," says Tim, echoing my feelings.

"This is just brutal. First, we can't attract any women, and now we have nearly failed all our courses. This just sucks."

I look for a ray of hope from some kind of Higher Power. "We'll survive somehow," I say.

Chapter 11

A THINKER

It is my second year in university.

I have decided not to stay in the dorm again.

My parents think that me staying in the dorm might have been a reason why my marks were so poor.

I stay at a house close to the university.

The house belongs to a friend of my parents named Deloris Jackson.

Delores is a very nice woman. She is nearly 70 years old, shorter and has a rosy complexion.

Another person staying at the house is Jim, who is in economics. Jim is about five feet nine inches tall and is very athletic. He has a car, but he hardly ever uses is. Most of the time he bikes everywhere he goes.

I admire Jim.

Jim is so disciplined. He studies for hours, reads the newspaper from cover to cover every day and listens to CBC all day.

I wish I was that disciplined. Again, the nerdier half of me wants me to be that way, but the cooler half of me wants to hang out with friends all the time.

After I come home from university, I sit on a sofa and talk to Deloris. Deloris sits comfortably in her chair with a book in hand.

"How was your day, Gaddy?" she asks. "Not that great," I say.

"Why is that?"

Deloris is so nice that I feel that I can tell her anything, which is what I do.

"I'm terrible at sciences," I say. "I thought things would go better in my second year, but they're not getting any better. I would do anything right now to be in the arts."

Deloris smiles.

"Gaddy, you strike me as more of a thinker," she says. "You seem like you are really meant for arts."

"I read other books besides my school work," I say. "I read all the great philosophers, and people like Carl Jung and Sigmund Freud. I really should be doing arts, but right now, there is nothing I can do. I'm stuck until the year is over."

"Hang in there Gaddy," says Deloris. Tim has moved into a new place as well.

He is staying in a basement suite in Vancouver. He is going to Langara College, and still hasn't told his parents about his grades.

I sit in the basement suite with Tim. It is very small. It has a table, two chairs, and two foamy mattresses to sleep on.

"How's school going?" asks Tim.

Tim has made a spaghetti dinner. It is delicious as we sit and eat and talk.

"Not very well," I say. "I really think I have made the wrong decision to be in the sciences."

"My courses are not going that well either," says Tim.

We watch a hockey game. After that, I decided to stay at Tim's place for the night. We both practically sleep on the floor.

During the weekend, in the morning, we study.

Tim usually plays music while we are studying. He is heavily into groups like Chicago and Bryan Adams.

The music is soothing and relaxing.

However, what I am studying still doesn't seem to be sticking in my brain.

I have brought one of Joseph Campbell's books, and I read it while I take a break from studying.

"Follow your bliss. That's what the books says," I say.

"You're reading something besides studying?" asks Tim. "Yeah. I am really interested in artsy stuff."

"Gaddy, you really should be in the arts."

"I know. But my parents say that you don't make any money doing arts. You need to become a doctor to lead a stable life."

"What about being a lawyer?" asks Tim. "You always gave great speeches in school. You would make a really good lawyer."

"Yeah, I guess," I say. "What about you Tim? Do you really want to be in the sciences.?"

"I don't like arts that much," he says. "I may not be doing that well in sciences, but I have to stick with it — I have no choice."

Later in the afternoon, we explore China Town in Vancouver.

Tim knows his way really well around Vancouver. He has such street smarts. I marvel at how he can go everywhere without getting lost.

"I wish I could figure out Vancouver like you have," I say to Tim.

"It's no big deal," he says.

"You must have been born with a great sense of direction." We stop at a small Chinese restaurant.

The place is a hole in the wall but the food is absolutely delicious. I feel lucky to be able to hang out with Tim and eat such amazing food.

We get back to Tim's place.

I then, take the bus back home to Deloris' place.

When I get home, I see her sitting again comfortably on her chair.

"Hey Gaddy," she asks, with a slight wave. "Hey, Mrs. Jackson," I say.

"How's everything going?" "Same as usual."

Deloris is watching the news.

"Did you hear about what happened in Los Angeles?" she asks. "No," I say.

The year is 1992.

"There have been riots on the street because of the Rodney King beating. It's so awful. It's so tragic what these people are going through."

I think for a moment how lucky I am not to be living in worse conditions — that I live in a safe place, where my family supports me.

Things may not be good, but they aren't that bad, I think.

Chapter 12

RELIGION

I am not extremely religious.

When it comes to my parents, they are not extremely religious either, even though my father was raised a Christian, while my mother was raised a Hindu.

My great uncle, who lived in India, was also a bishop in a Christian church.

One day, in one of my classes, I meet a girl who is from Prince George. Her name is Laura. She is Into-Canadian, and pretty. She has short black hair and a beautiful complexion. It turns out that our parents know each other.

I ask Dad about it on the phone. He says that he had a fight with Laura's dad, and that they stopped speaking to each other.

Regardless, I am interested in Laura. We seem to have a lot in common, especially because we have the same roots.

I go to visit Laura at her dorm.

We talk for a little while. I really want to ask her out. Suddenly, though, she asks me about whether or not I am religious.

"Are you Christian?" she asks.

"Um," I say, "not heavily Christian. My father was raised a Christian, but we don't attend church all the time."

"My Christian group is having a meeting," she says. "Would you like to come?"

I am not quite sure what to make of this.

I like Laura a lot, but I feel that the only purpose she has here is to convert me to her religion.

However, I like Laura, and I am curious about what this group is like.

"Yeah, I guess I can come," I say.

"Do come, I'm sure you will find it interesting," she says, smiling.

After visiting with Laura, I go to visit Bob for a bit. He is still living on campus.

Bob is heavily atheist. I am curious about what he thinks about Laura inviting me to a Christian group meeting.

"She may be trying to convert you," says Bob. Bob smiles.

He then says, "I would like to attend a meeting like that, and tell them what I believe in. It would probably lead to an interesting discussion."

"I agree with you Bob," I say. "I figure if I attend it will be at least an interesting experience."

A few days later, I attend the meeting.

There are about ten people in the meeting room.

All the people there greet me warmly. But I figure that there must something behind it.

A man stands in front of the room.

He is about six feet tall, skinny and has red hair and freckles.

His name is Daniel.

"So how is everybody today?" he asks. Everybody says fine.

"I would like to welcome a guest to our meeting today, Gaddy Das," he says.

Everybody says hello to me.

"Glad to have you, Gaddy," he says. Soon the meeting begins.

"It is very important that the only religion you should follow is Christianity," Daniel says.

"There are no other true religions in our world."

"We must serve Christ always, and always know that Jesus is the son of our Lord.

"We must spread the gospel everywhere. We need to be all over the city and all over campus, converting people everywhere. The more we convert the happier our lives will be."

Daniel pauses.

He then asks, "Did any of you convert anybody else?"

One of the female members of the group says, "I think I may have converted a few more. It's hard to tell, but I am hoping they have really understood how important being a Christian is."

The whole group nods in agreement.

After the meeting is over, Daniel acknowledges me again. "Thank you for coming, Gaddy. I hope you can attend our future meetings."

"Thanks," I say.

Laura later asks me how I found the meeting. "It was fine," I said.

"Will you come for the next one?" she asks. "I'll think about it."

Later, I talk to Bob about the meeting. "It sounds like a cult," I say.

"That's probably what it is," says Bob.

"I really like Laura, but this is crazy — this is definitely, not worth it."

"Smart choice dude," says Bob. Bob then smiles.

"I might want to attend that meeting just to have an argument with them about religion. It would be very interesting."

"Be my guest Bob," I say.

Chapter 13

WORKING OUT

Summer has arrived.

The regular school year has ended.

I have barely passed most of my courses.

However, I am happy after talking to my parents on the phone. They have agreed to me taking arts courses, and going into something else.

"I guess you maybe just weren't meant for that," my mother says.

"I don't know what else to think," I say. "I really studied as hard as I could, and nothing good came out of it." I will be taking some summer courses.

I will be taking a poetry course and a political science course. I tell Deloris how happy I am.

"I can't believe I'm finally going to do something I really enjoy," I say.

"Good for you Gaddy," she says. "I know things will definitely end up getting much better for you."

I will have to move out of Deloris' place during the summer because she doesn't accept borders then.

I decide to stay for the summer in another dormitory on campus called St. Andrews.

It's very peaceful and quiet there, especially during the summer. My parents come down to Vancouver to help me move.

My dad doesn't say much about my changing over to arts.

However, I know things will get better, and that my parents will be proud of me once again.

I have suddenly discovered something new in my life as well. I have a bike my parents bought me, which I have been using quite a bit. I decide one day to take a risk and bike down to one of the gyms at U. B. C.

I feel afraid and intimidated about going.

But, in the end, I decide I have to do this or else my life will never improve.

I get to the gym.

I take a deep breath, and walk inside.

It is a small gymnasium. There are a lot of huge guys banging and clanging the weights around. Guys are doing squats and bench pressing and using the heavy weights on the machines.

I slip into a corner of the gym where there is a bike, and I bike for a few minutes.

I'm sweating not because of the workout but because of the people around me.

There are also some women there all decked out in fancy workout clothes.

I finally decide to try one of the machines.

The machine works my shoulders and my deltoids.

I push and pull, feeling the strain of the weight against my body. I decide I will only work on this machine today.

When I am finished my workout, which isn't very long, I bike back to St. Andrews.

I am as sore as I can be.

I go buy something to eat from a cafeteria nearby, and I come back to my room.

I am sore all over.

But I feel so happy I finally did this. I continue to go to the gym every day.

I look in the mirror, and I notice how different my body looks. I am not scrawny anymore. I am bigger and fitter than I have ever been in my entire life.

The voices, which I usually hear, say negative things about me, start saying complimentary things about me.

"He is so handsome," they say. "He's such a stud."

I notice that women look at me differently now. They seem to smile more, and they appear more flirtatious around me.

My parents come to visit again, and they notice my appearance. "Well done with working out," says my dad.

"Thanks", I say.

"You look really good," says my mother.

Despite all this, there is something that I can't figure out. I always thought women were much less superficial than men when it came to the appearance of the opposite sex.

In the end, I realize that men and women are the same.

I think, though, why can' t people be loved for their personality rather than their physical appearance?

This seems so superficial.

Being a nice person should be the most important thing in life, rather than worrying about how you look all the time.

I realize I am healthier though, which is a good thing.

I remember so many years ago, when I was teased about my physical appearance, remembering how unattractive I felt.

However, I'm glad I worked out otherwise, I would never have known what working out was like. I felt great admiration for my bravery as well, not being afraid to step in the gym despite all those scary jocks hanging out there.

Chapter 14

CREATIVITY

While I am doing courses for the summer, and living at St. Andrews, I meet a woman named Jane, who is staying across from me.

Jane is a beautiful woman with a lovely smile. Her ancestry is Thai and British.

She is a journalist and is staying at St. Andrews for the summer on sabbatical before she goes back to her job in Thailand.

I tell Jane I am doing a poetry course for the summer. She seems very interested in this.

"What kind of poems are you studying?" she asks.

"All kinds of poetry, especially modern poetry," I say. "We're reading poems by Ezra Pound, William Carlos Williams, Wallace Stevens, and Leonard Cohen."

I tell her that I feel that anyone could have written some of the poems I am studying.

"You're missing the point," she says. "What do you mean?" I ask.

"This poetry you are studying is what creativity is all about. Yes, it may seem very simplistic, but their writing is all about experimenting and being creative."

I ponder over what she is saying.

"Maybe I should create my own poetry," I say.

"If that inspires you to be creative, then that is a good thing.

Everybody should be creative in their lives," says Jane.

Jane also overhears me playing violin.

I play a bit of the Four Seasons by Vivaldi, then I play something improvised by me that sounds quite weird and strange, I think.

Jane asks, "What were you playing?"

"I was playing some of the Four Seasons by Vivaldi," I say. "No, not that," she says.

"I was wondering about the other stuff you were playing."

"It was just something I made up. I was just having a little bit of fun."

"You should do more of that," she says, "rather than playing the old and familiar classics."

Jane makes me think about John Lennon of the Beatles when he married Yoko Ono.

Some people don't think Yoko Ono is as good an artist as John Lennon. The stuff she created is considered by some to be bizarre and lacking in tonality.

However, some call her art some of the most experimental art ever created. Other artists I know about are people like John Cage who created a piece called four minutes and 33 seconds, where the orchestra sits without playing anything for that amount of time.

Jane also has a brother named Don, who is a rock musician.

Jane asks me to come to a nudist beach in Vancouver to meet her brother.

Don is a tall man with long black hair. He truly looks like a rock musician.

Most of the people at the beach are hippies. They sit around playing guitars and singing 1960's songs.

I wear pants and a t-shirt down there, making me look a little out of place.

"Don, this is Gaddy Das," Jane says. "Hi, nice to meet you," says Don.

Don lies down on the sand stretched out, while Jane and I sit beside him.

"I'm selling shirts here. Do you want any?" he asks.

"No, I'm fine Don," I say.

We start to converse about all sorts of different things, including skiing.

"Yeah, I like snowboarding," says Don.

"I like skiing," I say, "but I'm no snowboarder."

Suddenly, he says, "This place is getting monotonous. I need to get out of this hippy colony."

Don then stands up.

"Let's go back to your place," he says to Jane. We all get up and head back to St. Andrews.

When we arrive in Jane's room, there is a guitar laying there. Don sits and picks up the guitar.

I sit across from him.

"This is a song called Forgiveness," he says.

Don starts to play. The guitar playing is amazing and his voice, a loud singing voice, booms across the dormitory.

I sit absolutely enthralled.

After playing, Don asks what I think. "That is amazing," I say.

I am amazed by Don, not only for his musical ability, but also because he has such a cool and mellow personality.

All I can think is this guy is meant for showbiz. "Thanks," says Don.

Jane's mother arrives a bit later.

She is the Thai half of Jane's ancestry.

She looks to be about in her seventies, and looks like Jane. She asks me to show Don where the bus depot is at U. B. C. "I don't want him to get lost," she says. "If you can take him there, that would be great." "No problem," I say.

I take Don to the bus depot.

"Thanks, Gaddy," he says. "Nice to have met you." "No problem Don."

In the end, I feel I have been truly inspired.

Chapter 15

COLONIALISM

After I have finished my courses at U. B. C., I return to Prince George.

I decide to cake courses at the local college called the College of New Caledonia.

While I am taking courses, I live with my parents. I decide to major in psychology.

I take several psychology courses, a sociology course, a history course, and an English course.

The college feels a lot more welcoming than U. B. C. It is smaller and everybody knows everybody else.

I like the teachers as well.

They are very easy going, and I find what I am doing to be a lot of fun, rather than a constant worry.

The course that I like most is English.

In English, we are reading the Heart of Darkness by Joseph Conrad.

The book is all about Colonialism, specifically about the colonization of Africa by Europe.

The book is dark and melancholic.

When I read it, it feels like watching an old black and white movie, something I really enjoy.

As for colonialism, I ponder over why it happens.

In Canada, the people who were the worst victims of colonialism were the Indigenous people.

The Indigenous people were the first settlers in North America.

When explorers from Europe showed up in Canada, they thought the Natives were savages that needed to be taught civility.

The Europeans took over the land that originally belonged to the Natives. And they treated the Natives with cruelty.

Why would somebody want to do this to somebody else? I ask myself.

If the Europeans simply thought we were all human beings, and that we are all equal, none of this would have even happened. The Natives, through no fault of their own, ended up living difficult lives.

Another thing I think is about is what happened in India when the British colonized that country.

British rule lasted for nearly 200 years.

The Indian people were treated badly by the British. Suddenly, out of nowhere appeared a hero named Mahatma Gandhi

Gandhi, peacefully, got the British out of India. He told the Indians to be self-sufficient, which was what led to the British downfall.

When it comes to colonialism, I think about myself as well.

I am an Indo-Canadian. I think how much racism existed, especially when I went to elementary school during the 1980s.

When my parents first came to Canada in the 1970s, they also put up with a lot of racism.

For a while, they lived in an apartment in Edmonton. My mum would cook Indian food.

She was told by the landlord that the food smelled awful, and she should stop cooking Indian food.

My dad told me, when I was younger, that I needed to work twice as hard to succeed in this country because my skin color was brown.

"You must work harder than the rest," he said. "And you must proud of who you are."

My parents, however, were not against me hanging out with white people. They had many friends who were white.

While in Prince George, most of my parents' friends were white.

However, we grew up with a different lifestyle than white people. We were told not to date when we were younger. Instead, our culture encouraged arranged marriage.

My parents, however, fell in love when they were younger, and didn't have an arranged marriage. However, they never dated anyone else before they met.

When I would watch television, all the characters on television were dating each other. I used to watch Three's Company and Happy Days, just to name a few.

Happy Days was all about dating and nothing else for the most part. I wanted to be like Richie Cunningham and the Fonz and date all the women in my classes, especially when I became an adolescent.

The boys in my elementary school would talk about girls all the time, while I had nothing to say on the matter. I also felt uncool because I came from a society that encouraged arranged marriage.

When I met Tim, who had the same problem I had, coming from a culture that didn't encourage dating, I found a kindred spirit. Despite that, the one thing, which I liked about our culture, when I was younger, was that our family spent a lot of time together.

We liked to travel together, eat meals together and, despite everything else, we enjoyed each other's company.

My parents were also more open-minded than a lot of others who had the same background.

My father had a record collection. Not only did he listen to a lot of Indian music, but he also listened to a lot of western classical music and rock music.

I discovered artists like the Beatles, Abba, Chicago, Neil Diamond, and the Monkees, from my father.

My mother also cooked non-Indian food.

She would make Indian food one day, and then the next day she would make pasta or burritos.

We grew up being very open-minded, which I think is a wonderful way to be.

All in all, being from a different culture had its ups and downs.

Chapter 16

SOLITUDE

When I am in Prince George, I have no close friends.

Tim is in Vancouver.

It is then I realize how wonderful solitude is.

I spend my days reading, studying, playing music and watching movies.

I go to the library in Prince George often. It is there, I borrow records of famous artists that I want to know more about and that I really enjoy.

I get Bob Dylan's greatest hits.

I listen to music, greatly inspired by its creativity. The music is poetic and beautiful. I also listen to the album, Revolver, by the Beatles. Again, the creativity and poetry of the album amaze me.

I enjoy rock music from the 1960s.

I am inspired by all the things that went on then, like the fight for civil rights, for democracy and gender equality

While I am in solitude, I can spend hours on this stuff, and I feel true enjoyment from doing it. Hanging out with Tim was fun, but the only problem was I felt like I was wasting my life.

However, despite all the beauty of solitude, there is one problem.

I hear voices.

I think that if I hear voices, I must be too alone.

The voices want me not to be alone.

The voices say, "You need to party more, and hang out more instead of being a hermit."

I am greatly inspired by monks.

They live in solitude, and they say they have found true happiness in solitude.

I am inspired by artists like Michelangelo and Leonardo Da Vinci, scientists like Isaac Newton and Albert Einstein who spent hours and hours alone.

I enjoy meditation.

Again, I feel this is the nerdy half of me, which believes in the benefits of solitude.

Besides studying, reading and listening to records, there is a piano in the house still so I continue to play piano, sometimes for hours.

The voices encourage me to hang out with friends and go to nightclubs and not come back home till late at night. I find this to be an extreme waste of time.

I picture myself going to a nightclub and trying to pick up women this way. I am not meant for this; I am against asking lots of women out. The guys I know who do that are considered desperate by women.

I enjoy watching a movie by myself on Friday night and having a banana split from Dairy Queen.

I am heavily into Alfred Hitchcock's movies. I enjoy movies like Psycho and North by Northwest. Most of my friends are not into anything like Alfred Hitchcock or when it comes to music, like the Beatles.

The movies nowadays, I find are often very gory and very violent. There is also a lot of swearing. One big star is Arnold Schwarzenegger. He is not really an actor; he is a bodybuilder.

Even though I work out a lot now, I don't want to be known for only being somebody who works out at the gym. I like movies that are intellectually stimulating and enjoy books that give me the same kind of stimulation.

Schwarzenegger is a terrible actor. And his movies are just a waste of time.

I read a lot of existential novels as well, including books by Jean-Paul Sartre and Albert Camus. These books deal with solitude, death and life. I identify strongly with these authors.

The Stranger, a book by Camus, talks about a man who doesn't get emotional about the death of his mother.

This may seem very disturbing, but I think the point Camus is making is that there is life beyond death, and even if your mother dies, you must continue to live.

Being in solitude has also helped me not to get attached to anyone or anything. This way of living can be found in the Baghavad Gita, a book from the religion of Hinduism.

Everyone will die, including you. You must accept that.

If you fail to realize that death is inevitable, you will end up leading a very miserable life.

Another thing I do in solitude is listen to 1930s and 40's radio comedy. I listen to legends of comedy, like Jack Benny, Red Skelton, George Burns and Gracie Allen, and Dean Martin and Jerry Louis.

Nobody, I know, who is my age, listens to this stuff.

Again, the comedy has an innocence about it and a brilliance as well.

I also listen to Woody Allen and Bob Newhart.

When I listen to their albums, it puts me into a deep, dark, relaxed mood. When you listen to their comedy, you almost feel like you are going into a trance.

The other comedy I watch is Monty Python.

Again, the comedy is so brilliant. I especially enjoy John Cleese, who also created Fawlty Towers, a truly amazing comedy show.

All of this stuff takes me away from wanting to attract lots of women, going to nightclubs, and being into very superficial things. The music nowadays, I still find like I did when I was younger,

is very superficial. It's always about sex and partying and nothing else.

The one thing that keeps me in the superficial world is working out. I work out every day, and that makes people think I'm not nerdy at all.

But really, I am a nerd at heart.

The voices, I hear, don't want me to be nerdy.

They want me to hang out and be like everybody else who is my age.

Here is a poem by the 18th-century poet Alexander Pope called 'On Solitude,' which I greatly enjoy.

'Happy the man, whose wish and care
A few paternal acres bound
Content to breathe his native
air In his own ground.

Whose herds with milk whose fields with
bread Where flocks supply him withattire,
Whose trees in summer yield
him shade In winter fire.

Blest who can unconcernedly find Hours,
days and years slide soft away; In health
of body, peace of mind Quiet by day

Sound sleep by night; study and ease
Together mixed; sweet recreation;
And innocence, which does
please, With meditation

Thus, let me live, unseen, unknown;
Thus, unlamented let me die;
Steal from the world and not a
stone Tell me where I lie.'

Chapter 17

FIGURINGOUTWOMEN

I discover, in the end, that I am happily single.

I don't need a woman to make me feel not lonely. I have some male friends who are the opposite.

They are the type that women very aptly call desperate.

They ask women out — sometimes numerous times. They don't accept no for an answer. They are desperate and lonely — a bad thing to be.

The most important thing in life is to be able to be by yourself. You need to, most importantly of all, like yourself, and like spending lots of time with yourself.

Even though I enjoy solitude, I am not alone.

People who are alone may have lots of friends, but they still feel alone.

When you are like me, women may find you more attractive. After I combed my hair in a neat hairstyle, and worked out, things which I didn't do a long time ago, women began to find me more attractive.

But the main thing about being attractive is not to be lonely and desperate.

Besides men who ask out women all the time, some of them sexually abuse women. To be attractive, you must not be desperate, lonely or abusive. You must treat women with respect and realize what they want in order to be attractive.

If you do meet your soulmate, that is a good thing.

But your soulmate needs to find you attractive as well as you finding him or her attractive.

Another term frequently used to describe certain men is the term bad boy. Men who are like this are supposedly attractive to women. To be in this category is not to be abusive or someone who can't take no for answer.

Men who are like this are very standoffish around women. They don't, or hardly ever, ask women out. They are a catch because they are not so desperate.

When you get up in the morning, you need to plan your day doing things that you enjoy doing. Don't plan your whole day to go to different places and ask all sorts of women out.

I avoid nightclubs.

Nightclubs are full of desperate, lonely men, and women who may enjoy turning these men down. When a man asks out one of these women, these women feel way more attractive, which increases their self-esteem.

The man, meanwhile, after being turned down, ends up having a lower self-esteem.

One of my friends, Roy, who I meet at the College of New Caledonia, is very good at attracting women. He wears stylish clothing and has a ponytail. He is very standoffish around women. In other words, when it comes to women, you need to talk to him, he doesn't need to talk to you.

Some of these desperate men think that men, who are more serious about themselves, lack a sense of humor when it comes to asking out women.

They believe they are meant to ask out women, and women are meant to turn them down.

This is a waste of time.

Instead of asking out women all the time, find something better to do with your time. Take up a new hobby, read way more, do something creative with your life.

I believe if you are meant to be with somebody, the Higher Power will help you find that person. Asking out one time is okay.

But when you get desperate and ask women out multiple times, you end up looking like a loser.

Working out is a good thing for me as well.

I am investing my time in trying to feel more attractive without asking out women. Being at the gym is all about you being into yourself, and not needing anybody else to reduce your loneliness.

You might not end up with a girlfriend, but you feel way better about yourself. Spending more time on yourself, and not worrying about having a girlfriend, is the best way to be.

Pop culture also tells you to ask women out all the time.

When you are down and lonely, and don't have a partner, pop culture tells you to feel miserable in being this way.

Great loners, like philosophers, artists, and scientists, are not mentioned in pop songs or, for the most part, on television. Trying to be like Leonardo Da Vinci, Isaac Newton, Jean-Paul Sartre or Friedrich Nietzsche is not encouraged in our society.

Pop songs constantly talk about solitude as being miserable, and they tell you that if you are not having sex all the time, you are a miserable person.

People who free themselves from this way of thinking feel much better about life.

They don't constantly need the opposite sex around them to feel true happiness.

I enjoy staying home on Friday night. I don't go to nightclubs.

I eat a banana split and watch Monty Python.

I feel great happiness in being this way. I know I am attractive, and I don't need anybody else to tell me so.

However, sometimes, I still hear voices telling me not to be alone, and to go out and party all the time. Despite hearing these voices, which come from the society around me, I try to ignore them.

Although I feel way more attractive, I am still vulnerable to hearing these voices — voices which I constantly have to ignore.

The only problem is these voices don't go away completely.

Chapter 18

EXISTENTIALISM

While I am in college, I read a lot of existential writing.

Generally, I have considered myself to be existential rather than religious.

There are several problems I have with religion.

One is that celibacy is greatly encouraged. You shouldn't overindulge in sex, but not having any at all, I think, can be unhealthy.

People shouldn't feel guilty about having sex. Sex is very human and is a very important part of our lives. When you make people guilty about their sex lives, they may end up having severe psychological problems.

The Bible encourages sexual activity only when you are married. This, I think, generally, is not a good thing. If people want to have sex outside of marriage, they should not feel guilty about it.

The Bible is also very male-centered.

Women are expected to only serve their husband and do nothing else. Women, I feel,

must be equal to men. They should be encouraged to both have careers and stay at home with children.

Gender equality, when it comes to pay, is very important. Women doing the same job as men should get equal pay. Women can do the same jobs that men do so they should be encouraged to work, as well as being allowed to stay home with children.

Men, similarly, should be allowed to be caregivers as well. Men should not be discouraged from being this way.

Another thing the Bible discourages is homosexuality. Homosexuality exists in our world — again, we cannot deny this. Homosexuals should be allowed to marry and have children.

When we realize that everybody is equal, it will make the world a better place.

Despite all of this, there are some positive things about religion too.

One thing is that religion encourages you to be compassionate to others. It encourages us to be kind to others and help others. If we follow the lives of Jesus, and the Buddha, for example, it is all about love and compassion for your fellow man.

Religion also encourages you to feed, clothe and build a shelter for the poor.

This again is very good.

When you help those, who are going through a difficult time, it makes you feel much better.

Existentialism can be followed while being moral.

However, religion talks a lot more about being moral, generally, than existentialism.

If you follow the 10 commandments, for the most part, you can lead a very happy life.

The other thing that religion talks about is an afterlife. What happens to you when you die?

Religion has an answer to that question, whether it be going to heaven or reincarnation. Some existentialists believe that once your life has ended on earth, it is completely over.

When you know where you are going after you die, you may end up having less fear.

The other thing religion does is encourage you to believe in a Higher Power. This is a good thing because if a Higher Power is with you, you fear less. Also, if there is a higher power watching over you all the time, you may feel the need to be more moral.

Pop culture generally is anti-religion. It encourages sex all the time.

Again, sex is healthy, on the one hand, but on the other, there is a lot of overindulgence. I think you should not feel guilty for having sex outside of marriage, but you will feel much happier if you don't have sex all the time.

Many rock musicians and actors lead very promiscuous lives, and they are our role models when we are children.

Rock music videos are full of sexual images.

When you spend all your time on sex, and nothing else, you end up leading a wasteful life.

Once again, however, the voices I hear, encourage me to be promiscuous.

"You should party, and be a rebel," the voices say. Again, I feel the conflict within myself when it comes to this.

The voices say everyone else is partying and having sex all the time, and you should too.

Having an Indian background, as well, I am encouraged not to date and not to have sex outside of marriage. My parents don't encourage me to do either.

When I work out, I start feeling more attractive, which increases my sexual appetite.

I hear friends around me, who are dating, talk about their fascinating sex lives. I feel left out from this.

I like to avoid nightclubs, and I like being in solitude, but sometimes I wonder what would happen if I went to a nightclub and ended up having sex at the end of the night.

What women wear, and their behavior, also greatly increases the sexual appetite. In the West, women are way more promiscuous.

They wear tight and skimpy clothing. Pornography is easily accessible as well.

Religion tries to discourage you from being into sex, which can be a difficult thing for some, but a good thing for others.

Religion encourages marriage, while pop culture encourages you to sleep around.

Why is there this conflict?

A conflict greatly felt by me.

If things were straightforward. when it comes to being sexually active, or only having sex when you are married, life would be so much easier.

In the end, all I can do is live in conflict, trying to figure out the society I am in.

Chapter 19

JOHN LENNON

I have finished attending the College of New Caledonia and am now taking courses at the University of Alberta in Edmonton.

I am continuing to do psychology.

I move to an apartment in Edmonton and live with my sister. My sister is a little shorter than I am and has a fair complexion. The apartment is right on campus, so my classes are nearby.

The one thing that is difficult to deal with in Edmonton is the extreme cold. I walk most of the time so I end up putting up with the cold a lot more than in Prince George.

The apartment has an exercise room with all the usual machines. I love working out there, and I try to work out as much as I can.

Besides doing courses, and working out, I become very interested in the life of my favorite Beatle, John Lennon.

I am very interested in Lennon's idea of peace. President Richard Nixon was after Lennon because of his anti-Vietnam protesting. Lennon, like many other artists throughout the world, was against the United States involvement in Vietnam.

Nixon was afraid that Lennon might rile people up against him. So, Nixon tried to have Lennon deported from the U.S.

I have the same views as Lennon about peace. Peace is very easy if we all want peace. It makes no sense for countries to be fighting with one another.

While I am working out, something interesting happens. I end up meeting a guy named George.

George is a short stocky guy with a ponytail. He was a hippy as well.

"How's your workout going?" he asks me. "Going well," I say.

"I have an injury so I cannot workout as much as I would like," he says. "You really look like you work out a lot," he adds.

George strikes me as an interesting character.

I am curious about his life as a hippy, especially because of my interest in John Lennon.

One day George invites me to his apartment to have a drink. George tells me he attended Woodstock during the sixties.

He remembers vividly his experience of hearing Jimi Hendrix. "We woke up, and suddenly this amazing guitar playing was happening," he said.

"The guitar was so mellow, beautiful and peaceful. It was just breathtaking," he says.

Despite being a hippy, George is not as much of Beatles fan as I expected. I ask him if he would like to watch John Lennon's video, Imagine, with me.

I get the video from a video store close by and come to his place the next day. George and I watch the video, and suddenly we both begin to sob.

"What an amazing man," says George. "I understand what he went through, trying to get peace in our world. I really identify with him."

Besides being a former Hippy, George is also a member of the Canadian Communist Party. George especially hates the United States.

"I wish somebody would blow the United States away," he says. "They think they are superior to everybody else. The people there are so ignorant about what is going on in the rest of the world."

George also talks about my Indian ancestry.

"India is a beautiful country. The people there are so amazing. I love Gandhi and all he stood for."

George has hardly anything to eat. He is extremely poor.

There is only one beer in his fridge, and no food.

George asks me if he can borrow some money to buy something to eat.

"I'm sorry to ask you, but I am desperate," he says. I lend him the money.

George is a sociologist and occasionally lectures at the university but makes very little money.

George is also very into women.

He looks at pornography all the time, and he asks just about every woman out that lives in our building.

Women fear George because George doesn't take no for an answer.

If George quit being so desperate, I figure he might attract more women because he has an interesting personality.

One day, I come to George's place to pick up the money he owes me. George had promised he would pay me back and told me to come and visit him.

I knock on the door. George answers.

George is flat out drunk.

George asks me what I am doing here.

"You told me to pick up the money you owed me," I say. George scowls at me.

"You don't give a shit about me," says George, "you just want your money. I thought you were different from everybody else, but you're no different."

George grabs a 20-dollar bill and hands it to me. "How miserable, life is so miserable," he says.

I notice a scar on his arm.

He obviously tried to kill himself. Tears come to my eyes briefly.

George then falls over on the floor — brutally drunk. I think he might threaten me so I leave.

George soon becomes one of my least favorite people.

Chapter 20

THE UNITED STATES

I am taking three courses with three amazing teachers.

One of the courses I am taking is a course in cognitive psychology.

The teacher is named Hal Johnson.

Hal Johnson's lectures are so entertaining they are like listening to stand-up comedy.

Hal says his greatest influences are Woody Allen and Jean-Paul Sartre.

Hal is short in stature and wears glasses, making him look a little like his idols.

He attended the University at Berkley in California.

He strikes me as having the same views I have. He is more existential, and very liberal.

He is for gender equality and gay rights.

Despite having such a wonderful teacher, my grades are not that good. I go to see Hal about my marks on my latest exam.

"What can I do for you?" he asks.

"Is there anything I can do differently on my next exam to improve my grade?" I ask.

"The teacher's assistant marks the exams," he says. "All I can recommend you do is study as hard as you can for the next exam. If things don't work out, there isn't much else I can recommend."

Suddenly, while I am with him, curiosity grips me.

"Did you attend Berkley?" I ask. "Yes, I did," he says.

"Alberta is so much different from Berkley," I say. "How did you end up here?"

"Alberta is fine," he says. "Alberta is generally a nice place.

You're right, though, they are way more conservative here."

I feel such a strong connection with him that I ask if he supports gay rights.

"Yes," he says. "Berkley is such a good place because they support equality for all. I miss Berkley when it comes to that."

He appears to be a little teary-eyed.

"You're a very good professor," I say. "I really enjoy your lectures."

"Thanks," he says, "It really makes me feel appreciated." Besides this course, I take another course in Religious Studies.

The teacher of this course, named Ron Howell, has a beard and glasses, and we have amazingly, interesting discussions during every class.

I raise my hand often feeling the need to say something because the discussions are so interesting.

"How can anybody walk on water, or turn water into wine?" I ask.

"This clearly shows that you can't believe in everything that religion teaches you."

Another student, a short Indian looking student, raises his hand.

He believes in religion literally.

"Those miracles did happen," he says. "You can' t say they didn't happen because you weren't there when it happened. If you don't believe in the Bible literally, you are going against the message of Christ."

I respond.

"You can be moral and not be Christian," I say. Ron interrupts our discussion.

"Can you really be moral and not be religious?" he asks. "What do you think?" I ask Ron.

"I'm not here to spout my views. I am just a moderator in this discussion," he says smiling.

Another debate we have is whether or not Jesus was a regular human rather than being a Christ figure.

"Jesus, may have lived," I say, "but never performed any miracles. The message Jesus sent to us about compassion and love may be his, but the idea of performing miracles may have been totally made up."

The same student responds to my statement.

"Jesus was not just another human being," he says. "He is the Son of God. If you don't believe this, then you don't really believe in Jesus."

Besides these classes, there is another class I really enjoy. It is a sociology course with a teacher named Jake Stewart.

Jake Stewart, who graduated from the University of Alberta during the sixties, is a partly bald man with a big figure.

In the class, we study about rumors, specifically ones to do with the Beatles. A rumor was spread, during the sixties, that Paul McCartney had died. John Lennon said in the song Strawberry Fields that Paul is dead.

Being such a huge Beatles fan, I am greatly enthralled that we are studying this in class.

"When I protested during the sixties, we really stood up for what we believed in," he says. "The sixties were such an amazing time to be alive. We fought for everything, including Civil Rights, equality for women and peace."

Despite the interesting courses I am taking, I began to feel something strange happening to me.

George keeps haunting me.

He is against the United States.

By befriending him, and having more liberal views, I think the United States might be after me. These amazing teachers also might be trying to send me subliminal messages to tell me that the United States is after me.

They know I am the key to overthrowing the evil conservatives in the United States.

Having the views, I have, they know that I might be able to rile people up, and have them protest against the United States.

The United States, I believe, is trying to overthrow every government in the world that doesn't support their views.

George, despite me not liking him much, might also have come to Edmonton to send subliminal messages to me to be against the United States.

Sometimes, I think this is true and at other times, I think it may not be.

Chapter 21

THE COUPLE

I am studying for a psychology exam.

I study as much as possible.

I take notes as I study, trying to remember everything I need to for the exam.

While I study, I start hearing voices from across the wall in my room.

"Yeah, I think he's studying," a man's voice says. "Still studying?" says a woman's voice.

"I remember when I was younger," says the man.

"All I ever did was party, smoke pot and listen to the Rolling Stones. He is so young. He should be out there partying. It seems like he has no fun — he has no friends."

"Bit of a nerd," says the woman.

I feel upset hearing what I am hearing.

An Australian couple lives next door to me. The man is short and stocky and wears sunglasses all the time, while the woman is a shorter, middle-aged, attractive woman. I figure they are bored, and they are eavesdropping on me. I feel upset that they are calling me lonely as well as calling me a nerd.

"I can hear you," I say.

"Oh, you can, can you?" says the man.

Suddenly, I hear classical music coming from the couple's apartment.

The man starts to laugh.

"You're so lonely," he says. "Don't you ever go out and party?

You're a young man. You should be out there enjoying your life." "I like being here," I say.

"You like studying this much? Studying is such a bore," says the man.

"I agree," says the woman. "Quit spying on me," I say.

"You're too alone," says the man. "When you are this alone, you are against the United States of America. We're spying on you because the United States has hired us to spy on you. You need to stop being alone — otherwise, we won't leave you alone."

"You're spying on me?" I ask. "Yes," says the man.

"Yes," echoes the woman.

"You're into John Lennon. This is something the United States is against. You need to be more social, have lots of friends, go out a lot, go to church. If you are the way you are, the United States will not leave you alone."

"What about George?" I ask.

"The United States is after George, as well," says the man. "He is having a bad influence on you. He is against the United States and has dangerous views against the United States."

"Look, I have to study so I won't fail everything. Will you please leave me alone?" I ask.

Suddenly, it sounds like somebody has turned up the classical music.

"Stop being a nerd," says the man. "Stop it," says the woman.

They begin to laugh. "Loosen up," says the man. "Leave me alone!" I say.

Suddenly, I start banging on the wall. "You jerk," I yell, "leave me alone!"

I bang so hard on the wall, that my fists nearly start to bleed. I then hear a louder voice.

"Quit banging on the wall," says a man's voice.

It sounds like the man's voice except much louder.

"Come outside," I say. "Do you want to fight? I'll beat the shit out of you."

The man says again, "Stop banging on the wall."

I go outside, standing in front of my apartment door as well as the couple's door.

Nobody comes out.

My sister is still in classes and hasn't come home yet. I wait for a few hours.

I then decide to go downstairs and workout. While I am in the gym, I see the man.

I am ready for a fight.

The man approaches and then stops a few inches away. "Are you okay?" he asks.

"Yeah, I'm fine," I say.

"Why were you banging on the wall?"

"You were bothering me. I heard stuff from across the wall." "I swear I didn't do anything," he says. "You have got the wrong guy."

"What do you mean?" I ask.

"This apartment is full of noise," he says. "The noise you heard may have been coming from upstairs. I complain about the noise quite often."

"Oh," I say.

"I'm sorry I did that," I say.

"Look if you have a problem with the noise, call the main office. But for goodness sake don't bang on the wall — I have pictures on that wall, and some of them came off the wall while you were banging it."

All I could now think is what in the world was I hearing?

Chapter 22

THE PSYCHIATRIST

My mother comes to stay over at our apartment.

I tell her about what happened with the Australian couple. My mother looks concerned.

"Are you okay?" she asks.

"I don't know," I say, "I may be hearing voices — I'm not sure." My mother talks to my dad over the phone.

My dad has medical friends in Edmonton. He is able to find me a psychiatrist.

I wonder if I need one or not. Maybe I'm hearing things, or maybe the couple was really spying on me.

The next day I go and see the psychiatrist.

His name is Dr. Jack Hardy. He is a shorter man with a beard and looks a little like Sigmund Freud.

"Hi," he says. "Do sit down."

"What appears to be the problem?" he asks gently. "I may be hearing voices," I say.

"What kind of voices?" he asks.

"I think I'm hearing a couple across from my apartment talking to me, telling me to quit being alone and quit being nerdy."

Dr. Hardy looks concerned. "Are you lonely?" he asks.

"I like being by myself," I say. "But what I'm hearing is that I should quit being by myself."

"Do you socialize much?" he asks.

"Not that much," I say. "But what's wrong with being alone?"

"If you feel alone, then you need to change something in your life. But you sound to me like you have some sort of conflict within yourself."

"You mean being alone or being social?" I ask.

"Yes. If you like being alone, you shouldn't be having any doubts about being alone. It's okay to be in solitude. But even people who have lots of friends can feel alone."

"I love solitude," I say. "I like not having to rely on others for company. I like to be as independent as possible. I love sitting by myself and reading or playing my violin or even studying."

"This happened to you when were you studying?" he asks.

"Yes," I say.

"You might want to take a break from studying. Are you worried about your grades?"

"I am worried."

Besides worrying about my grades in my courses, I am also thinking about applying for law school.

"Worrying about your grades may be causing you stress," he says. "You probably need a little more break time."

"Okay," I say. "I'll try to take more breaks."

I add, "I never go out on Friday night like everybody else. I work out on Friday and do laundry and stuff like that. The voices seem to be asking me to go out especially on Friday."

"Do you have any close friends?" he asks.

"Not really — not now anyway. But I really like being by myself."

"All I can recommend is taking a break," he says. "If you need to socialize, you need to find some way of doing that. But otherwise, all I can recommend is that you relax a bit more, which may reduce your stress level."

"Thanks," I say.

I say goodbye to Dr. Hardy, and leave the office.

In a few days, I will also be writing my law school entrance exam, known as LSAT.

I have been writing old LSAT exams. I hate this exam, and I am doing very poorly at it. I fear that I may not be able to get into law school because of my poor performance.

I write the exam.

A few weeks later, I receive my marks. I receive a very low mark on the exam.

I am angry and shaken. I apply to several law schools in Canada, but I don't get in anywhere.

Suddenly, I hear that my dad, who is having problems with the healthcare system in Canada, wants to move from Prince George.

He goes to the United States and looks for jobs there. Eventually, he decides he would like to move to Alabama — specifically Winfield, Alabama. My mum agrees and they decide to move.

My mum calls me and tells me about the move. "We're going there in a few months," she says.

Then an idea dawns on me. Maybe I can move to Alabama, be closer to my parents, and apply for law school in the United States.

I also think that my teachers at the University of Alberta, who I think are against the United States, are sending me subliminal messages, trying to get me to move to the United States — specifically Alabama. My parents, I think, are receiving subliminal messages as well to move to Alabama.

If I get into law school in the southern United States, I could become a politician and change Alabama from being a backward place to being a progressive place.

Civil Rights, and equal rights for women and gay people, are things I strongly believe in. People in the South, I believe, have been conditioned by evil politicians and leaders to be against black people and homosexuals.

Before I leave Edmonton, I am watching rock music videos on television. I see Don, the rock musician from Vancouver, on television in a rock music video with his own rock group.

I am so amazed that I buy his rock group's album and write a fan letter to him about peace.

In the letter, I talk about John Lennon, and his battle against the United States.

"Do write a peace song," I say in the letter to Don.

"We need to bring back John Lennon in any way we can. The United States is trying to colonize the world, being against any government that doesn't support them.

"We need to change the world, and especially, the United States in any way we can."

Chapter 23

ALABAMA

I still hear the same voices in Edmonton coming from the Australian couple.

Instead of getting angry this time, I ignore the voices and don't react to them.

Also, before I move to Alabama, I phone Tim, telling him that I am moving to the United States, and that we will not see each other for a while.

"Oh," says Tim.

"I will be moving in a few days," I say. "Oh well," says Tim. "That's too bad." Tears start to fill my eyes.

"I really enjoyed our friendship," I say. "Thanks, Gaddy," he says.

"You may want to come and visit me, if you like," I say. "No problem," says Tim.

"Take care."

A few days later, I am busy packing my stuff. I don't have that much stuff, which I am grateful for. I pack one duffle bag, which I will take to the United States. I am greatly looking forward to moving, experiencing a new place, discovering new things.

I finally get on the plane.

After a few flight changes, I arrive in Alabama.

My sister and my parents are there to greet me. My sister will leave in a few days to go back to Edmonton to stay in an apartment by herself. Despite liking each other, my hearing voices put my sister in a tough situation.

I got up one night and started yelling at the voices.

My sister had a test the next day and was afraid she wouldn't be able to go to sleep.

My sister was not pleased, despite what I was going through. However, I realized how difficult it must have been for her to put up with this.

My parents are happy to see me. "Welcome to Alabama," my mum says. "How are you guys liking it so far ?" I ask. "We really love it," says my mum.

"The people are so friendly here, and it is such a beautiful place as well."

We drive from the airport in Birmingham to Winfield. Along the way, people wave from their cars as we drive by. "Very friendly, don't you think?" says my father.

"Very friendly," I say, being amazed that people who don't even know you wave to you from their cars.

We finally arrive at our house.

The house is not as big as the one in Prince George, but it is a fair size.

That evening we go out to dinner at a steak place in Winfield.

The steaks are delicious, and we drink lots of ice tea, or sweet tea as it is called in Alabama.

A few days later, my sister leaves for Edmonton.

Meanwhile, I have been accepted at the University of Alabama which is in Tuscaloosa. I can't wait to start school.

Before starting university, I get a tour of the campus. I am amazed at the history of the university. This is where Civil Rights took place, where black students, at one time, were prevented from going to university.

Despite integration, the university is still, in a way, segregated. The black students only hang out with the black students, for the most part, while the white students only hang out with the white students.

I wonder why they can't just come together.

Despite integration, white students still believe in the Confederacy. They, however, say they preach history not hate.

However, if you look at the history of the South, it is really about nothing but hate.

While I am touring the campus, I also meet a guy from Kuwait named Saddam.

Saddam, who is also a foreign exchange student like me, is a big, burly man.

He wears glasses and is slightly balding

He says he was a bodybuilder in Kuwait and took part in competitions there.

"Do come to visit sometime," he says, "if you would like." I agree to do that. He seems very friendly.

I still have thoughts about what I am going to do in Alabama, while I am here. Despite being integrated, there is still discrimination against blacks and also especially against homosexuals.

There is a letter to the editor written in the school newspaper, saying hateful things about homosexuals. The language is graphic, and I can't believe they allow something like this to be published.

I feel a need to stand up for the rights of those who are oppressed.

I write a letter to the paper, condemning the hateful letter.

I show my father in Winfield, the letter. My father is not so enthusiastic about me having the letter published.

"We're in a different place," he says. "I am afraid of what might happen to you if you get this letter published. It may be very dangerous."

I am surprised by my father's reaction.

"But this is against what I believe in," I say.

However, despite that, I start to fear for my safety. The Ku Klux Klan has deep roots in the South. Although I am not happy about it, I decide to take my father's advice, and not publish the letter.

Chapter 24

UNIVERSITYOFALABAMA

Despite all my political battles, academics is going well for me. I'm taking a full load of courses in communication studies, which I hope will get me into law school in the United States.

One of the courses I am taking is an American Studies course. The course has a lot of the history of rock music. I enjoy learning more about my favorite artists like the Beatles and Bob Dylan. I want to be like my favorite artists and change the world.

However, despite all of that, I know my political views are against the state of Alabama.

Admiring artists like Bob Dylan and the Beatles, especially when it comes to John Lennon, I think could be dangerous.

John Lennon is anti-religious. Just about everybody in Alabama belongs to the Christian church and are greatly against existentialism.

I begin to think that the Alabama government, and the federal government of the United States, might be after me. I remember George and his hatred of the United States. It is possible that the United States may be after George as well.

I am convinced I have received subliminal messages from my teachers in Canada to get me to the United States, specifically Alabama, to fight against the conservatives and change the United States.

Many politicians in the United States, especially the conservatives, want every other country in the world to support their government. The Central Intelligence Agency, or the C. I. A., I think, is trying secretly to overthrow any government that is against the United States.

While I take courses at the University of Alabama, I still think my teachers, who I think are against the conservatives in the United States, are trying to send me subliminal messages in order to make states like Alabama more progressive rather than backward. The way to do this is to get into law school, especially the University of Alabama, and become a politician. I am a good speaker, and I think I might be able to persuade those in the South to quit being so backward.

My first semester goes very well. I receive straight A's and end up on the honor roll. I study for hours, not doing much else. I also enjoy watching the football team at the University play during the weekends.

I am starting to hear voices again, though.

The voices have changed from the couple I used to hear to voices from those around me in Alabama. I try to ignore the voices, but I am starting to think that may be the United States government has gotten in on my voices.

There is also a group at the University of Alabama who wants the South to separate from the rest of the country. I think they may be connected to the government and might possibly be after me because of my political views.

Other than Saddam, I don't have any close friends.

I like solitude, but I think that being in solitude might be too liberal for Alabama. In the apartment I am staying at, there are parties every weekend. Most of the students' party all the time, go to church and belong to a fraternity.

I feel like an outsider.

Also, there is hardly anybody who is my skin color at the university.

Saddam, interestingly enough, also like George, hates the United States.

"America is bad," he says. "Sometimes I wish I wasn't here. "You don't know that right away, though. But the people here are so superficial and are immoral. The United States is the enemy of the world. They think they are superior to everybody else. You meet an American, and you realize how ignorant they are about the rest of the world."

I agree with Saddam.

"It's true America is very ignorant," I say. "All they know about is their own country. They don't even want to know about the rest of the world."

I begin to think that the United States may be after Saddam as well.

Through the television, the United States government may also have sent me and Saddam subliminal messages to lure us to Alabama. They want us here so they can screw us up and stop us from convincing those in the United States to be more liberal.

One day I am driving home from school.

I hear voices that are telling me that the state of Alabama is after me.

I ignore the voices. However, suddenly, I feel a choking sensation on my neck. I began to fear that the Alabama government is trying to kill me.

"We don't like your type down here," the voices say.

"You're against the state of Alabama and the United States.

We'll scare the bejesus out of you," they say.

I stop my car.

I get out of the car. I am in front of a dentist's office. I go inside.

There is a receptionist there. I ask her to call 911. She asks what's wrong, and I say I feel like I am choking.

She calls 911 and an ambulance arrives. I am taken to a hospital in Tuscaloosa.

I see a doctor at the hospital.

The doctor asks if he can contact someone who is either a friend or a relative. I ask them to phone my parents.

I am scared out of my wits.

What the hell is going on? I wonder.

Chapter 25

SCARED

My parents show up at thehospital.

They are not pleased with my behavior. "What the hell are you doing?" asks my dad.

"They are after me," I say, "the Alabama government is after me."

"What?" asks my dad.

"They are after me. They don't want me to change Alabama.

They think I am a threat to their way of life."

My mother, despite being upset as well, realizes that I might need to see a psychiatrist.

"I think we need to find a doctor for him to talk to," my mother says.

"You mean he may be mentally ill?" asks my dad. "Yes, that's the only thing that makes sense here."

Again, my dad has medical connections in Alabama, and soon finds me a psychiatrist.

A few hours later, my parents drive me to the psychiatrist's office.

We enter the office and the secretary tells us to have a seat. I am still afraid for my life.

"I really need to be somewhere, where somebody can watch me all day," I say. "I am so afraid that they are going to kill me."

My parents look astonished and worried.

They now sit quietly and say nothing. The psychiatrist comes out of his office.

He is an older looking man with a greyish beard. Again, like the last psychiatrist I saw,

he reminds me a little of Sigmund Freud. "Come in," he says to me.

He tells my parents that he will be back in a little bit. He shuts the door.

"Please sit down," he says. "Your name is Gaddy?" he asks. "Yes," I say.

"I'm Doctor Bill Hayes," he says, smiling a little. "What seems to be the problem?

"I think the government of the United States and the government of Alabama are after me."

"Why is that?" he asks.

"They think I am a threat to Alabama's way of life. I am too liberal, and they are afraid I might influence those living in Alabama to become more liberal. Then the conservative politicians would lose hold of their power over the citizens living in the South."

"Are you on any medication?" "No," I say.

"It looks like I may have to get you to an institution."

"I don't care where I go, as long as somebody is watching me all the time so they don't kill me."

"Have you been feeling any major stress lately?" "Not any different than before."

"Are you in university or have a job?"

"I am attending the University of Alabama."

"You might need to take a break from your courses," he says. "The stress may be what is causing you to think what you are thinking."

"Do you mind if I call your parents back in here?" "No, go ahead."

He opens the door and summons my parents into the office. My parents both have worried looks on their faces.

"He needs to be institutionalized," he says to my parents. "He is obviously hearing voices, and he may have some form of schizophrenia."

My mother, after pausing for a while, finally says something. "We had something like this happen before when he was living in Edmonton, attending university there," she says. "He was hearing voices there too. But the doctor there didn't really do much for him while he was there."

"He is probably stressed out as well," says Dr. Hayes. "He needs to take a break from studying and feel better."

"No problem," says my dad. "We'll do whatever we can to help him."

We leave Dr. Hayes office, and we drive to a psychiatric hospital close by.

My parents escort me into the building.

A nurse who is short and chubby with a rosy complexion is there to greet us.

"Your name?" she asks. "Gaddy Das," I say.

My parents look worried.

"You can leave him here — he'll be fine," says the nurse. "We'll take good care of him."

"Are you okay?" asks my mother.

"Yes, I'll be fine. I'm much safer here than anywhere else," I say.

My parents hug me and then leave, both of them slightly teary eyed.

"Take your clothes off and put this gown on," says the nurse. I do as I am told.

The nurse shows me my room.

I am sharing a room with another psychiatric patient.

He is quite elderly and frail and looks like he may have dementia.

There is a curtain that separates us.

"The lounge is here," says the nurse escorting me there.

The lounge is filled with people who look totally out of it. Some are sleeping, while others are awake with blank looks of their faces.

I still hear voices.

"We got you," says a voice. I fear for my life.

Chapter 26

THE PSYCHIATRIC WARD

I sit in the lounge of the psychiatric ward.

I have been here for a day. Nothing has happened to me. I am not dead. I feel relieved about this.

However, I start to hear different voices. "He's such a loser," says one of the voices.

"He doesn't even have a job, and he's not attending a university. He's so lazy."

I don't respond to the voices. Despite these voices being a pain in the neck, at least they are not threatening to kill me.

I stare at the other patients.

Most of them are sitting down in chairs, stuck in their own world. Many of them speak, but their words are slurred, and it is difficult to understand what they're saying.

A black man, who looks to be in his twenties, approaches me. "Hey brother," he says. "Can I borrow your toothbrush?"

I try to ignore him.

"Jesus loves you brother," he says. "Believe in Jesus, the son of the Lord."

Despite being in a psychiatric ward, I still don't think I am insane. I am not totally out of it like many of the other patients.

A psychiatrist shows up.

He wears glasses and has grey hair.

I am one of the patients he is supposed to see.

"My name is Howard Meeks," he says to me. "Do step into my office."

I take a seat.

"What seems to be the problem?" he asks. "I am hearing voices," I say.

"What are they saying?"

"Before it was the government of the Untied United States and the government of Alabama wanting to creep me out and kill me. Now I'm hearing voices criticizing me because I don' t have a job, and I am not attending a university. The voices say I'm lazy."

"I think you need to be put on some sort of medication," he says. "I can prescribe Zyprexa for you."

"What does that do?" I ask.

"It may help you to get rid of the voices." Suddenly, I feel scared.

"I don't want to take any medicine," I say. "It might have side effects."

"You are required to take it. It will help you with your problem.

If you don't take the medicine, you won't get any better." I sit silently for a few minutes.

"I guess there's nothing else I can do," I say.

"You are required to take at least one pill daily," he says. "Okay," I say reluctantly.

After the meeting is over, I head back to the lounge. The same nurse as I saw before comes to greet me.

"Here is your medicine," she says, holding out her hand. "Thanks," I say.

I swallow the pill, drinking a lot of water with it.

I am scared again. Maybe this is what the United States wanted to happen to me. Once they could prove I was insane, and get me on psychiatric medication, there is no way I could succeed politically in Alabama.

This may be why I stopped hearing their voices.

Suddenly, a voice says, "We got you. You're finished. You can't do anything now."

This voice then goes away, and I keep hearing voices telling me what a loser I am and how lazy I am.

As I am sitting in the lounge, I notice a pool table in front of me. There is an elderly man shooting pool by himself. I ask him if he wants to play a game. He agrees.

After playing on the pool for about half an hour, I think the psychiatric ward isn't as bad as I thought it would be.

However, I start to feel bored, and despite it not being that bad, I still want to get out of there as soon as possible.

Suddenly, I hear a woman screaming. "You bitch," she yells.

It's a female patient yelling at one of the nurses.

"I don't want that fucking medicine," she says. "You can't make me take it.'

"I hate you," she says.

After the screaming dies down, a nurse asks us to line up for lunch.

"Lunch is served," she says. "We'll be having fish and chips."

The food isn't great, but it isn't that bad. After a few days, my parents come to visit me. "How are you doing?" asks my mother.

"I'm fine. I'd like to get out of here as soon as possible," I say. "This place is really kind of dreary and boring."

"The psychiatrist said you are doing better and they will release you in a few days."

"Just hang in there," adds my father.

I hug them both. I miss my mother's cooking, and a nice bed to sleep on, as well as being able to go outside when I want to.

However, there's not much I can do right now.

Chapter 27

REGRETS

I am finally allowed to come home.

I am so relieved to get out of the psychiatric ward.

My parents come and pick me up and drive me from Tuscaloosa to Winfield.

After about an hour, we reach the house in Winfield.

My parents have gotten a dog as well. The dog is a Great Dane. The dog barks at me, at first, not knowing who I am. But after a while, she stops barking. Her name is Maggie, and she is such a beautiful looking dog.

"How are you feeling?" asks my mother.

"Feeling better, now that I have gotten out of the madhouse." My dad, my mother and I sit down at a table in the kitchen. My mother makes tea.

I drink the tea and feel such relief to be home again.

"You will have to take some time off from school," she says. "Yes, the psychiatrist told me that," I say.

I start hearing voices, voices telling me that I am lazy for leaving the university and not having a job.

The voices, I think, come from people who live in Winfield. "What a loser," say the voices.

Despite hearing the voices, I ignore them. I realize that if I get angry at the voices again, I could end up back at the psychiatric ward.

After I have tea, I take a nap.

In my bedroom, I begin to think about what it would be like if my life were normal if, like other people my age, I had lots of friends and partied every weekend.

I wondered what it would be like to live here and go to church every Sunday and join a fraternity.

Why am I so by myself?

I ponder as to why I seem to embrace solitude so much. I think solitude is glorious, but the world doesn't seem to want me to live in solitude.

Everywhere, on television, in magazines, in books, everybody is encouraging me to be social. I should go out to nightclubs every weekend and have a steady girlfriend. I should never be alone because being alone is supposedly dangerous for your mental health.

I think people are after me because, through being alone, I am a threat to their way of life. I then start to think about geniuses who lived in solitude. Whether it be Henry David Thoreau, or Leonardo Da Vinci, they embraced solitude, and they recommended it as a good way to live.

I then start to miss Tim.

At least I had one close friend back then. Maybe if I had continued to hang out with him, none of this would have happened. Yes, I hear voices, but if I had close friends, maybe the voices wouldn't bother me as much.

I begin to regret being so into existentialism.

Maybe I should have been more religious and gone to church. Even though a lot of the stuff that people in the church do seem a little weird to me, if I went to church, I might not be so alone, and that the voices would get better.

I remember George as well, and how miserable he was.

He was more by himself than me and was heavily into existentialism.

Maybe this is why he was so miserable.

While I am staying in Winfield, I read a book called The Purpose Driven Life written by Rick Warren. The book is all about being a Christian and how glorious life is.

Warren says Christianity is the only true religion to believe in. He encourages people to go to church and be social with other Christians. He also is in support of converting other people to Christianity.

I think about maybe joining a church, but in the end, I decide not to.

However, what does appeal to me about religion is that encourages being compassionate and kind to others.

I hear voices now saying that "he is so lonely. He doesn't have any friends. He is so by himself."

My parents have a lot of books in the house. I read a lot while I am in Winfield.

I also read a book by the Dalai Lama.

The book talks about Buddhism and being compassionate to others. I believe in what the Dalai Lama says. I believe being kind to others is what life is for, and that this is truly a great thing to believe in.

I also read books by the famous Indian writer, J. Krishnamurthi. He holds a totally different view from Rick Warren when it comes to solitude. He believes that being in solitude is a good thing, and also, he believes in something called the religious mind, which talks about having compassion for others.

I wonder what it would be like to be dating and having a great social life.

However, I still feel that that kind of life is so superficial. All normal people my age worry about is how they look, what clothes they wear, working out, and how many parties they attend.

I am so not like this.

But sometimes, I have regrets.

Maybe being a normal sociable teenager, and a normal sociable adult, is the key to leading a happier life.

Chapter 28

LAZY BUM

I sit on a couch in our house in a room filled with books. "God, he's so lazy," says a voice.

He sounds like some elderly man in Alabama.

"I remember when I was younger, if I ever did what he did, I would get a good whooping. Kids, or adult children, are so spoiled nowadays," he says.

I feel like a loser.

I have no job, and I'm not attending university. I have the misfortune of being called an adult child, a child who still needs to be looked after by his parents.

While I am at home, my parents decide to invite some guests over for a small gathering.

As the people arrive, I see everyone talking to each other. They laugh and they make small talk.

I stand by myself, or near my parents, the whole time. No one will talk to me. I begin to think that they think I'm just some loser, who lives at home with parents. Or that I am a rich doctor's kid, spoiled rotten by his parents.

After the gathering is over, I help my parents with the dishes. I then think why can't

these people realize that I am a good person, that hearing some voices isn't my fault. These people are so ignorant — they don't have a clue what I'm going through.

I occasionally leave the house to go for a walk in a park nearby, or to go and lift weights.

I am very by myself now.

I hear a voice say, "He must be on drugs. These spoiled, rich children are all on drugs."

"His parents should kick him out of the house," a voice says. "He doesn't deserve any better. If I were his dad, I would let him know who's boss. He should fend for himself and quit being so spoiled."

My parents and some friends decide to go on a trip to Italy.

My parents say they really want me to come with them, and they would prefer if I didn't stay home all alone.

"Do come," says my mother. "I don't know," I say.

"If would be better if you came." she says. "if anything happens to you, we will be able to look after you."

My dad agrees.

"Do come," he says.

Eventually, I agree to go with them. I am still a little frightened of some of the scary voices I have been hearing.

A few days later, we fly to Italy.

We stay in a posh hotel, and we tour Italy with other people.

All of the guests on the bus, except for a few people, are alumni of the University of Alabama.

I hear a voice say, "He looks really spoiled. I want to see his dad get tough with him, show him who's boss. I can't wait for them to start arguing."

We tour Rome as well as some other cities on the bus.

While I am in the hotel room, and occasionally on the bus, I read a book about Michelangelo.

He was a loner, the book says. I figure also that reading the book makes me look studious, rather than like some of kind of drug addict who is dependent on his parents.

Another voice, a woman's voice, says, "He needs to grow up.

He still needs his mommy."

"I'm sure he is a drug addict," says a man's voice. "Probably the type that could end up in jail."

As we tour Rome, we see The Colosseum, as well as St. Peter's Basilica. We also visit where Michelangelo did some of his most famous works, like the Sistine Chapel.

I am really interested in seeing these things.

I have a great admiration for geniuses in Italy, like Michelangelo, Leonardo Da Vinci,

Raphael and composers like Rossini and Vivaldi.

I want to really be like them, be a creative person, and enjoy solitude.

Another voice says, "Why doesn't he have a girlfriend? He should be chasing after women like any young man his age."

These people on the bus with me seem less interested in Rome and more interested in showing off how wealthy and snooty they are.

I hear voices saying we have worked so hard to get where we have gotten and have never been spoiled in our entire lives.

Nobody on the bus talks to me.

They all talk to each other and with my parents.

I really envy my parents in this situation. They fit in with this group. They are both doctors, well educated, have a lot of money, have children. Nearly all the people on the bus are their age as well.

Then there is the generation thing, as I like to refer to it.

The Baby Boomers, I think, are saying, he is just a spoiled Generation X kid.

"Typical Gen X'er. He's bumming off his parents," says a voice. "He's probably never worked a day in his life."

I start to think about my Caucasian friends in Prince George. They all had jobs during the summer. Their parents, I figure, were a lot like the people I hear on the bus.

I can imagine hearing their voices, telling their kids how lazy they were.

"You have a kid, you don't spoil him," a voice says.

"I'm still tougher than my son. If we get into a fight, I can still whoop his ass," a voice says laughing.

Another voice on the bus says, "His parents should make him work. He needs a good, old fashioned job is what he needs."

These people don't realize that I am not lazy. I am a good person.

Unfortunately, I was born with the parents I have, and I also hear voices through no fault of my own.

I want people to think I am a good person, not some spoiled, rotten, rich bum.

While I am deeply interested in Italy, these people seem to be only interested in being snooty and stuck up. I would welcome a conversation with them about Italian architecture or painting or music.

Instead, they don't see me that way.

They just see me as some spoiled, skirt chaser who doesn't care about anyone, especially his parents.

Chapter 29

WRITING

After spending a few months at home, I finally go back to university and complete my psychologydegree.

I then apply to a few law schools in the States, but I don't get in. Unfortunately, my LSAT score is not high enough. I decide not to redo the LSAT, thinking that I will end up with the same score even if I do it over again.

Eventually, however, I find something that I am good at, and that could land me a career.

I really enjoy writing.

Even if I don't write perfectly all the time, I still love sitting down in front of a computer and typing my thoughts out.

I read a lot as well, which helps me become a better writer. Even though I can't be a doctor or a lawyer, I still have writing

— maybe I could become a journalist instead.

I am not familiar, at first, with all the rules of journalism. So, I read some books about it. I also read lots of newspaper articles in order to get better at journalism.

Also, I take a course in journalism at the University of Alabama. I find out that many journalists don't have journalism degrees.

The way to become a better writer is to read and write a lot.

I write stuff in a computer diary. Here is some of my writing:

-Solitude-

Solitude is a glorious thing. I enjoy being myself, and doing things in solitude. I enjoy writing and music especially.

Writing and music are similar in many ways. Being a good writer, or a good musician, requires having a good ear. You need to hear your writing to be a good writer. The writing should flow. The way to develop flow as a writer is to read good writing, whether it be Hemingway, Sir Arthur Conan Doyle, or the journalist Jules Loh.

To be a good writer, as well, you need to write every day. When you write every day, you start to improve. Writing, like music, also requires editing. When you correct mistakes in writing is like when you learn to hit the correct notes in music

Writing is generally a solitary activity. If you enjoy solitude, you may enjoy writing way more. After I finish writing, I look forward to editing. Editing requires a fine-tuned ear. You need to hear your writing to make it better.

I try to read and write for a few hours every day. When I read, I look for writing, which sounds musical. When you read musical writing, it is very gentle on the ear. The words flow, which makes it easier to read.

—Reading-

Reading is a very relaxing activity.

If you are a writer, however, you need to pay close attention to what you read, and take the good from it, rather than the bad.

Besides reading books, I read lots of newspaper articles as well. A good news story both entertains and informs the reader. When you read a good writing style, you feel like you want to read more stuff like this.

A good journalist also asks good questions. When it comes to questioning somebody, you need to ask questions from a reader's perspective. Assume the reader knows nothing about the topic you are writing about. Ask as many questions as possible to make things as clear as possible.

After you have done that, then write your story, putting in bits and phrases you have from your interview.

The writing should be concise and easy to understand.

This is the key to good journalism.

I enjoy taking the journalism course at the University of Alabama.

I still hear voices, but finding myself has made my voices better.

One voice says, "He is a good man."

Another says, "He's also good looking. He really is putting an effort into becoming a good person."

However, another voice says that I'm still too lonely, and that I need more friends. Despite that, I feel much better and am easily able to put up with that voice.

I also follow the news way more, something I hadn't done as much before. I enjoy watching CNN especially. News I think is all about morality. When people do bad things like murder or steal, they get reported on the news.

The idea, I think, behind the news is to realize that you shouldn't do bad things in order to lead a better life.

However, many say that the news is also heavily reliant on ratings.

If a story is very shocking, it will draw more viewers in.

While I am in Tuscaloosa, I stay at an apartment at my parent's friends son's place.

I love studying journalism, as well as just writing in general.

Unlike when I did sciences, I understand everything that I am studying, and I also realize that it could lead me to having a career.

The only regret, I have, is that I didn't study journalism in the first place when I entered university.

I hear a voice that says, "His parents have spent so much on him. He is really lucky to be able to continue at the university."

My journalism teacher, named Rick Jones, is a very interesting character. Besides having a Ph.D. in journalism, he has worked in all sorts of different newspapers, including the Mobile Register in Mobile, Alabama, and the Orlando Sentinel in Orlando, Florida.

He is tall, wears glasses and is slightly balding.

"The key to being a good journalist," he says, "is to be able to write concisely and simply.

"Simple, concise writing is what people want to read."

I am, at this time, also looking for a job in journalism, and I ask him for his help.

After making a few phone calls, he recommends that I go to Selma Alabama, and see if I can get a job at the Selma Times Journal.

He knows the editor there, and recommends me for the job.

I am extremely happy. Finally, things are starting to get better.

Chapter 30

SELMA

After finishing the course, I drive over to Selma for a job interview at the newspaper.

There is hardly anybody on the highway leading there. The drive is pleasant. It's also a very sunny that day, making everything look bright and green.

When I arrive at the newspaper, I see something that nearly brings tears to my eyes. Right across from the newspaper is the famous Edmund Pettus Bridge, where Martin Luther King Jr., and many other protesters, marched to gain equal rights.

I take a glimpse at it, and start to picture the marchers crossing the bridge and being harassed by police. It is not a huge bridge. I imagine the pain that the marchers must have felt when they were hosed down by police.

They were such good people fighting for such a noble cause. I enter the newspaper building.

"Hello, can I help you?" asks a secretary. She is African American and very attractive. She has a beautiful complexion and dark brown eyes.

"I'm here to see the editor," I say. "Follow me," she says.

I follow her back towards the editor's office.

The backroom has a few computers in it. There I see several journalists typing things on their computers.

The editor's office sits directly in front of where all the computers are.

I walk inside the editor's office.

The editor is sitting in his chair, reading newspaper articles. "Thanks Gertrude," he says.

The editor is medium height and wears glasses. He looks about 30 years old and looks to me to be the type to be attractive to women.

"Hello," he says. "Do sit down." I sit in the chair opposite him.

"Could you ttell me your name again?" "Gaddy Das."

"Nice to meet you, Gaddy. My name is Howard Ramsay."

"I have a recommendation from Dr. Jones asking me to hire you," he says.

"Yes," I say.

"I really respect Dr. Jones. He was one of my favorite teachers.

A recommendation from him carries a lot of weight with me."

After asking a few more questions, Ramsay offers to take me to lunch.

We go to lunch at a restaurant nearby. It looks like an old-fashioned place made mainly out of wood.

The assistant editor also comes with us. She is Caucasian, tall and pretty.

"My name is Norma Johnson," she says to me.

"My name is Gaddy Das," I say. "Nice to meet you."

We sit at the restaurant and talk about Dr. Jones as well as what my job in Selma will be like.

"There is never a break here," says Ramsay. "We are always working. It's not an easy job since so much is going on here. But if you are looking to get a great experience in working, and in being a journalist, you can' t get any better than this."

"Yeah, we have so much to do." echoes Johnson. "It's pretty stressful sometimes."

After finishing lunch, we go back to the newspaper.

Ramsay gives me an assignment to do to test my journalistic ability.

It is a story on mayflies in Selma.

I am asked to phone an expert on bugs as well as asking the City of Selma what they think about all the mayflies flying around in the summer in Selma.

I do the assignment with ease, and I enjoy myself as well. A few days later, Ramsay tells me that I have the job.

I am thrilled. I hear voices again, but these voices are all positive.

"He's so smart, and so good looking," says a woman's voice. "He'll make a great journalist," says another voice.

I arrive in Selma a few days later, and find a house to rent. The house is beautiful, and is in the rich part of Selma, where there are old stylish houses.

Selma is like being in two different worlds.

There is the white world and there is the black world.

The houses on the other side of town are all run down and miserable. People living in the black half of Selma are all poor. Most of the prison population is made up of black inmates as well.

The schools in the black area are not as posh as the ones in the white area.

Even though segregation has ended, the black people and the white people all choose to go to separate schools.

In the newspaper, there are some black journalists and white journalists. They see each other during the day, but they never really hang out with each other after work.

Having my skin color, I am a man who is in between both worlds. To the satisfaction of my editor, I gain the trust of the black people and the white people.

The newspaper prints a headline one day saying, "Selma From Civil War to Civil Rights."

The white half of the town talks about the history of the South, where they say it is all about heritage and not about hate.

Meanwhile the black half talk about getting the vote, the segregation that went on here, and the oppression they have suffered forever.

I drive to work every day and see that bridge and think how much further we have to go for true equality to take place, and for everybody to live together as one.

In the end, I wonder to myself if this really is the world that Martin Luther King envisioned?

Chapter 31

WHITE AND BLACK

While I work at the newspaper, I cover all sorts of different beats. There are not that many journalists so I get to cover a lot of stuff.

My favorite beat is the crime beat. Every morning, I go to the police station in Selma and read the crime reports. I then usually meet with the chief of detectives who gives me the information I need in order to write a story.

The chief of detectives is a short, mustachioed man named Harry Bentley.

"Like that story, you wrote yesterday," says Bentley. "Thanks Chief," I say.

"As long as we get good coverage, I am a happy camper. These policemen work so hard, and deserve all the credit that they can get," he says.

Most of the offenses I write are about are drug offences.

Occasionally, there are a few murders, and there are lots of thefts.

Most of the inmates are black.

Selma, I think, represents the United States as it really is. It is all about white privilege and black oppression.

Most of the blacks were born into slavery, a period of that should be looked upon as a bad time to be alive. The whites say, however, that this heritage must be preserved in history. It is as though they are not sorry about what happened back then.

Other beats I cover, include the education beat, the city council as well as occasionally writing some lifestyle stories.

I really enjoy my job.

I finally have come to terms for not making it into med school or law school. I realize that I am born with other talents. The Higher Power, I believe, blesses us with different talents, and it is our job to figure out what they are.

Despite everything going well, however, things slowly begin to take a wrong turn again.

I'm still hearing voices.

Suddenly, one day, while at a council meeting, I hear a threatening voice.

"We gave you the chance to integrate with the white people," the voice says. "You are siding way more with the black people. You are still a rabble-rouser, and you want to take away our white privilege. We rule this country, and you had better respect that."

I go home, and the voices continue to haunt me. I go to work the next day.

I am starting to feel the choking sensation again.

I put up with it, desperately wanting not to lose my job. I sit at the computer, hearing the voices taunting me.

"You are against the white people of the United States," says a voice. "You are a threat to our way of life. We won't allow you to destroy our way of life."

The voice further says, "The articles you are writing are against the white people of this State and this country. We will not allow you to continue doing what you are doing."

At lunchtime, I come home and lie in bed.

The voices are beginning to get so distracting that I don't think I can go back to work. I get up feeling tired.

Despite that, I push myself to get up and go back to work. However, while at work, I start to get distracted and whisper, when hopefully nobody is watching, to the voices.

"Leave me alone," I say. "I haven't done anything wrong."

"I don't think so," says a voice.

"I am not against the white people of Alabama," I say.

"Yes, you are," the voice says. "You are just born that way — I swear."

The voices tell me that just by looking at someone's behavior, you can tell if they are liberal or conservative.

"Conservatives don't get angry in public," says the voice. "They smile and they bullshit way more. Their writing is way more complex rather than being simplistic and easy to understand.

"Liberals are angrier, and they write in simple plain language.

They don't bullshit. You fit this category," says the voice. Suddenly, I start to feel the choking sensation again. I finally have to leave work and go home.

"I'm sorry," I say to the voices. I am now really frightened.

"I'll quit being liberal," I say. "Please don't kill me."

"I don't want you working here anymore," says the voice. "Besides that, you got rich parents, they can take good care of you. You don't need to work — you're spoiled rotten and you deserve what you get."

I am angry, but I am too frightened to respond angrily to the voices.

I lay in bed.

The phone rings.

I know it is the newspaper wondering where I am. I don't answer the phone.

I call my parents.

My dad picks up the phone.

"Dad, I'm feeling really sick again," I say. "I need you to come get me."

My Dad, despite the horror of the situation, stays very calm. Being a surgeon, I figure, must help with that.

"Are you okay?" he asks. "Please come and get me," I say.

"Okay Gaddy," he says. "I'll be there in a bit."

After a few hours of lying in the dark, hearing these scary voices, I hear a knock at the door.

My dad has finally arrived.

Chapter 32

THE ARGUMENT

I open the front door.

My dad is standing there. "Are you okay?" he asks.

"I'm scared — I'm hearing things again," I say. "Okay, I'll take you home," he says.

We get into the car. My dad and I drive back to Winfield. We don't say much to each other on the trip there.

Once we reach the house, we go inside.

My mum is sitting on a chair in the kitchen. Her head is slightly buried in her hands.

"Are you okay?" she asks.

"I'm not feeling very well," I say. "I need to get some rest." "Go ahead and sleep," says my mother, "we'll talk in the morning."

I go to a room that really belongs to me, even though I have not been living in Winfield.

I change for bed, and lie down. I hear the voices again.

"You're finished," says a voice. "You will not intrude on our way of life. You're too liberal, and you're a rabble-rouser."

The choking sensation has stopped.

I lie down and reflect on what has happened. Despite feeling scared, I eventually fall asleep.

The next day I wake up. I find out that the newspaper has fired me from my job. I feel miserable. There is nothing I can do. Maybe the voices are right — I am finished for good this time.

I sit with my parents at the dinner table in the morning.

"We have to keep paying rent on the house," my mother says. "The woman, who owns it, won't let us get out of our contract with her."

"I'm sorry," I say.

"What are you going to do now?" asks my mother. I sense the disappointment in her voice.

"Everything was going so well there for a while," she says. "What happens now?"

"All I can do is rest here, and get better," I say. "Maybe after a little while, when things get better, I can try to reapply for some other jobs."

"What are you going to do while your here?" she asks. "All I can do is read and take it easy."

My mother then says something that ticks me off.

"You need to get a haircut," she says. "You're starting to look like Sai Baba."

Sai Baba is a religious leader in India. Referring to his looks and comparing them to the way I look is obviously meant as an insult.

"What?" I say.

My dad echoes my mother's sentiment. "Gaddy, you really need a haircut," he says. "My hair is just fine," I say.

"No, it isn't," says my mother. Suddenly, I get up from my chair. "You're being a jerk," I say.

"Don't talk to you r r mother that way!" says my father. "Fuck you!" I say.

Suddenly, my dad gets out of his chair.

"Get out," he says. "I want you out of the house." There is a small pause.

I am now extremely angry. I know the voices are going to start telling me again that I am being babied by my parents. Everybody in Winfield will think the same thing, and I will have to put up with this nonsense again.

In the end, I really want to leave and be on my own. I don't want to be some spoiled, rotten adult child. I am not that way. I can take care of myself — I don't need anybody else's help.

I figure my parents are betting that I will give in and not leave. I get up and go to my room.

I pack my stuff.

I tell my dad to fuck off.

He yells at me saying, "Get Out!"

I leave. At this point, I don't care where I end up. I would rather die than be considered a spoiled, rotten, adult child again.

There is a car outside that belongs to me. I get in the car and take off.

Where I will end up, God only knows. I am so angry.

I drive very fast, not caring if I ran into someone. Because I am so angry, I don't fear anything.

Even if I don't have any money left, I will not come back home. I would rather starve than put up with stupid nonsense from the voices, my parents and the people in Winfield.

Chapter 33

MISSISSIPPI

I drive to Tuscaloosa.

I stop there for the night at a small motel.

The motel looks kind of rundown, and I think there may be some scary characters lurking around there.

However, again because I am so angry, I don't care whether I live or die. I have faced death before but not this much.

I check my bank account.

My parents haven't taken the money out of the account. I wonder, for a while, why they haven't. Maybe they are still concerned about me, despite what happened between us.

I am hungry. I order a pizza to be delivered to my motel room. I can already taste the mushrooms and pepperoni. This will be the best pizza I have ever tasted. There is a small television in the motel room, which smells like cigarette smoke.

It is then I begin to hear the voices again.

"He's such a bad boy," says a woman's voice. "He's such a rebel. He doesn't need his parents."

Despite the craziness of the situation, I realize that the voices want me more to be like this rather than the other way. I suddenly don't feel so abnormal anymore. I am not some spoiled, adult child.

I am a rebel — and I can survive on my own. There is a knock at the door.

I open the door, and a delivery guy, a pimply-faced man, hands me my pizza.

I pay with my debit card, still wondering when the money will run out.

I am also low on gas. I figure I will get a little more gas tomorrow and see how long it will last me. After eating the pizza, I feel tired, but not tired enough to go to sleep.

I think about my life, and where I go from here.

Soon, morning approaches, and I have hardly slept a wink.

I check out of the motel, and start driving to only who knows where. I soon reach the Alabama Mississippi border. I keep driving. I am not used to driving for a long time on crowded highways. I feel a little scared, but again the anger gets rid of the fear.

Eventually, I reach West Point, Mississippi. I'm running really low on gas.

I stop at a parking lot near a pizza place and a video store.

It is dark and rainy outside. I decide I will have to sleep in the car for the night. That way I won't waste money on finding a place. I start to feel hungry. The video store looks like they might be hiring. I have never had a job, other than at the newspaper, in my entire life.

I walk into the store.

There is a tall, clean-shaven man, who looks about 20, who stands at the service counter.

"Hi," I say.

"Hello."

"Are you guys hiring?" "No, we aren't," he says.

I explain my situation to him.

"I am out of money, and I am homeless. I really need some way to make money in order to survive."

Surprisingly, he seems very understanding.

He takes forty dollars out of his pocket, and hands it to me. "Here you go," he says, "that should last you a while." "Thank you," I say absolutely astonished.

I then leave the video store. Across the street, there is a Subway restaurant. I walk over there and buy a sandwich. I sit at the restaurant and eat the sandwich. Because I am so hungry, the sandwich is heavenly — it is the best thing I have ever eaten.

Afterward, I go back to my car.

I get in the back of the car, and sit. While sitting, I fall asleep. I wake up in the morning.

I get out of the car. I feel well-rested but still a little hungry.

I look across the street. There is a Huddle House Pancake house. I decide to walk over there to see if they are hiring.

I walk in and ask to see the manager.

A short man with curly hair comes out to meet me. "Are you hiring?" I ask.

"Yes," he says.

"Do you need a dishwasher?" I ask. "Yeah, we could use one."

"I am homeless right now, and have no money left. I really need to work otherwise I won't survive."

"No problem," he says.

"Do you have a place to stay for now?" "No, I don't."

"I can probably put you up at my mother's place until you find a place."

"Thank you," I say.

"What's your name?" he asks. "Gaddy Das."

"My name is Bill Phillips."

After conversing, I go back across the street and park my automobile at the Huddle House.

"When can you start?" asks Phillips. "I can start right now," I say.

He shows me how to use the dishwasher. I often did dishes for my parents at home so this won't be too much of a challenge.

He then hands me a Huddle House t-shirt. "You can wear this," he says.

I find doing dishes to be worthwhile.

The voices start to say what a rebel I am, and that I am capable of taking care of myself.

"He's such a bad boy," says a woman's voice. "He's so brave," says another voice.

After work is finished, Phillips takes me to his mother's house. "Hi my name is Donna Phillips," she says. She is an attractive woman who looks to be in her fifties.

"You can stay here until you find a place," she says.

"Thank you, I say. "You have both treated me so well. I wouldn't have been able to survive without you."

"No problem," she says.

She shows me to my room. The house is very dingy and has dog poop on the carpet. Despite that, I am grateful just to have found a place.

She allows me to eat dinner with her as well. She makes spaghetti and meatballs.

I am so hungry that I devour everything very quickly. We talk for a short while about my situation.

"I will allow you to stay awhile," she says, "but you have to find a new place."

Night comes, and I go to my room and fall asleep. I have never eaten or slept so well in my entire life.

Chapter 34

GIRLFRIEND

The next morning, I get up.

I greet Donna in the kitchen.

I thank her for allowing me to stay at her place. "No problem," she says, "it was nice having you." "I will start looking for another place," I say.

I then get in my car and drive to work at the Huddle House. I see Bill sitting in his office.

He smiles at me as I greet him. "Thanks Bill, for all your help," I say. "No problem Gaddy," he says.

He then looks at me and pauses for a second.

"If you need to stay somewhere temporarily, there is a motel close by," he says.

I thank Bill for his recommendation.

I then get to work. Bill says it is okay to have a drink of lemonade if I am thirsty. We also are allowed to eat the food from the Huddle House for either lunch, dinner or breakfast without having to pay for it, depending on when our shift is.

It is a very hot day.

I drink a lot of lemonade.

Today, I work the afternoon shift and the evening shift.

Doing dishes at a restaurant is a very repetitive thing. However, it also gives me a great sense of accomplishment. Also, just being independent gives me a sense of accomplishment.

During the evening shift, a young black woman comes into the restaurant with a friend and orders dinner.

The woman is very attractive. She has a beautiful smile and a lovely complexion. She is wearing a t-shirt and blue jeans.

Suddenly, the voices, which I still continue to hear, tell me to take a risk.

"Ask her out," says a woman's voice. "Take a risk — don't be afraid."

I decide that taking a risk might not be a bad idea. I took a risk and left my parent's place, and now I feel so much better about myself. Maybe taking another risk will again be a good thing.

I go to her table. I take a risk.

"Hi, my name is Gaddy Das. Would you like to go out with me?" I ask her.

She smiles and starts to giggle. "Go out with you?" she asks. "Yeah," I say.

She then pauses for a bit and then smiles shyly at me. "Sure, I guess that would be alright," she says.

She gives me her phone number, and tells me to call her sometime.

"My name is Ashley James," she says. "Nice to meet you, Ashely," I say. "Nice to meet you as well."

Later, after Ashley leaves, and my shift is over, I drive to the motel that Bill recommended. It is a small motel, very rundown. The bathroom is dingy, and the bed is sagging. It looks too good for even a cockroach to stay in.

But I am feeling so good about being independent that I don't worry about the conditions I am in.

I decide to call Ashley the next day.

I'm feeling so happy. She said yes. She must really find me attractive. After all, I have been through, I feel on top of the world.

I go to sleep that night in the saggy bed. I sleep soundly after a hard day's work. Bill has also paid me — so the next morning I go and deposit the money in a bank account.

I'm not making a lot of money, but what I have I can live on. I eat very frugally. I have discovered a new way of living. Maybe someday I could write a book about how to live on nothing.

Later, that evening, I call Ashley. "Hello," she says.

"Hi, this is Gaddy, the guy you met at the restaurant yesterday." "Hi Gaddy," she says.

"Would you like to go out this evening?" "Yeah sure," she says.

She tells me to meet her at a Chinese restaurant close to where she lives.

When I show up there, I see her standing in front of the restaurant. She is wearing jeans and a t-shirt again. She smiles at me as I approach her.

We go inside the restaurant.

We sit at a table. The restaurant is not super fancy, but that doesn't bother me. I am so happy to have a girlfriend, finally.

I start to tell her about what happened to me, and how I ended up in West Point.

I mention my parents and how much I despise them for saying what they said to me.

"Who needs parents?" I say.

Ashely, however, is not entirely convinced of this. "Your parents must be really worried," she says. "Ah, yes, I guess so," I say.

"You should give your mother a call."

I sit, somewhat awestruck, with what Ashley has said.

I figure women wanted me to be independent of my parents. When I hung out with my parents, I kept hearing women's voices telling me I was not independent enough.

I am beginning to wonder what the real deal is here.

I tell Ashley, however, that I will phone my parents. After dinner, we go to Ashley's apartment.

We end up having sex that night.

It feels so good to finally feel more normal. I have a job; I live by myself and I have a girlfriend. Life is really worth living. Despite having little money, and sleeping in a horrible place, I feel happy as can be.

However, despite that, I still do begin to wonder if my parents are okay.

Chapter 35

THE DETECTIVE

I get up the next morning and head to work.

I have some breakfast at the Huddle House. I have some pancakes with maple syrup.

Anything I eat now tastes so delicious because I am eating so much less.

I think about finding a newspaper in West Point, where I can use my journalistic skills. I ask people where the newspaper is. After driving around a little bit, I eventually find the location.

I park the car and go inside.

The office is medium-sized, and has several computers. I ask to see the general manager.

I wait for a few moments until he arrives.

He is an older man who wears glasses and has grey hair. "What can I do for you?" he asks.

"HI, my name is Gaddy Das. I am looking for a job as a part-time reporter. Do you have anything available?"

"Have you worked as a journalist before?" he asks. "Yes. I worked at the Selma Times Journal in Alabama." "Yeah, I think we could use a little help," he says.

"Do you need anybody right away?" I ask.

"Yes. Come back tomorrow, and we'll see what we can do."

"Thanks," I say.

I leave the newspaper and head back to the motel. It is the afternoon, and I decide I will call Ashley. I dial the number. A voice on the other end says this number no longer exists.

I wonder what happened.

Maybe Ashley thought things were moving too fast, and didn't want to see me again. However, I can't quite come to terms with this, considering that our date seemed to go so well.

For some reason, Ashley got scared of me.

I walk across the street from the motel and grab a coffee. Coffee is very inexpensive, and is very tasty, especially when you are very thirsty and hungry.

I drink a lot of coffee. However, I don't eat very healthy. A voice tells me that I don't need to eat healthy food. The voice says you should eat for pleasure — that is what real health is.

"Eating sugar is what makes you healthy," says the voice. "You have been lied to by people, telling you that vegetables are healthier than ice cream. Ice cream is way healthier."

I think about this, and it starts to make sense. Stuff that tastes good should be healthier than stuff that tastes horrible. It seems only logical that this is the truth.

I have also heard of people, who are very healthy and who have had heart attacks.

While I am at the gas station, I also buy a chocolate bar, and have this for lunch.

Also, since I am eating way less, this must be healthier as well, I figure.

I go back to the motel room.

There is a television with only one channel in the room. I watch television.

Night soon approaches.

All of a sudden, I hear a knock on the door. Lights are flashing from a car into my room.

I feel quite scared about answering the door at night, especially in a place like this. Despite that, I take a deep breath and open the door. Standing outside is a tall man in a trench coat with a large mustache.

"Hi, are you Gaddy Das?" the man asks. "Yes, I am," I say.

"Your parents are outside. They hired me to look for you. I am a detective."

"They're outside?" I ask.

I realize that my parents are really worried about me. However, I thought they were angry at me, and didn't want to see me again.

"Your mum wants to talk to you," he says. "Would that be alright?"

"Yes," I say, "That'll be fine."

The detective goes to get my mom.

My mum looks tired, like she hasn't slept much in days. "Hi Gaddy," she says.

"Hi," I say.

"Your dad and I really miss you. We're sorry about what happened. We want you to come home."

I pause for a second.

"Are you sure? You really ticked me off with what you said."
"Yes, your father is really worried. I am too. We need you to come back."

I think about it.

I start to empathize with my parents. They really must be worried about me, possibly thinking that I might get hurt or even get murdered by someone.

After a few minutes, I tell her that I will come home.

"I have to quit my jobs first," I say. "Once I do that, I will come home."

"Can you meet us at the Olive Garden in Tuscaloosa tomorrow for lunch?" she says.

"Yeah, that would be fine," I say.

My mother gives me a hug, and tells me that she is glad to have me home.

I feel sorry for them. They have been good parents most of the time. I figure it is time I returned home, and stopped being so angry.

Chapter 36

HOME

The next day I wake up.

It is kind of a relief to be leaving this motel. I stare at the dreary walls and the dingy bathroom and I wonder how I was able to stay here for even this long.

The other thing is I constantly felt hungry and thirsty. Finally, I will have regular meals again, and start to feel better.

The only thing I worry about is that I will lose some of the independence I felt while being in Mississippi. I had a girlfriend, a job and my own money to live on. When I move back in with my parents, I might hear the voices I heard before.

I pack everything, get in my car and drive to Tuscaloosa. It is lunchtime.

I head into the Olive Garden restaurant. My parents are already there.

I sit across from them.

"How are you doing Gaddy?" asks my mother. "I'm fine," I say.

My dad doesn't say much, but I can tell he is very happy to have me home.

"So, you got a job there," says my mother.

"Yeah, I was working at Huddle House restaurant," I say. "I didn't make a lot of money, but I could survive with what I had. I also applied for a job at the newspaper there."

"You are very self-sufficient," says my mother. "I'm proud of you."

"Yeah, I, more or less, proved to myself that I could survive on my own. I wasn't sure about doing that, at first, but now I realize I can."

I order some fettuccine alfredo.

The food is delicious. There are definitely some advantages to coming home. I also miss my mother's cooking.

At the end of the meal, my dad pays for lunch. It is then that I hear voices again.

"He's relying on his parents," says a voice. "He must be a spoiled, adult child."

"No doubt — he's a spoiled, rich kid with rich parents."

It is then I consider whether or not I should tell my parents that I would like to go back to Mississippi.

I think about it for a while. However, I realize how worried my parents would be. I feel a great sense of empathy for them. They have worked so hard to give me and my sister a good life. Immigrating from another country is not easy. The thing they value most is their children.

I feel miserable with the idea of leaving them for good. And I don't want them to worry about me.

The other thing is the conditions I was living in were miserable. There just doesn't seem to be any point to living like that forever.

My parents have also apologized for what they said. So, I would not be in conflict with them if I moved back home.

When I get home to Winfield, I phone the Huddle House as well as the manager at the paper.

I tell them both that I am quitting.

Both of them sound happy that I am going home.

"You went to university," says Bill. "You really are overqualified to be a dishwasher."

"Thanks, Bill, for all you help," I say. "No problem, glad to have met you." "Thanks," I say.

I drive back to Winfield, following my parents. When I get there, I unpack my things and start to settle in. I now realize that I need to find another job. I want to work as a journalist again. However, this time I will have my parents' consent, rather than them worrying about me.

I lay on my bed in my room and rest. I then go out for a bit to the Walmart in Winfield.

While there, I shop for some music.

I purchase the Beatles anthology which has a few CDs in it. It has some Beatles music that I have never heard before. I am excited to be able to listen to it.

I go home and listen to it, the soothing voices, the beautiful music that is so rich with creativity.

I especially listen to John Lennon, my favorite Beatle. It is then, I hear a voice.

"Gaddy," says the voice. "Yes."

"I'm still alive," "What?" I say.

"You were meant to purchase this album." "I was never assassinated," says the voice. "I faked my assassination."

I then realize who I am talking to. It is the voice of John Lennon. I am listening to a 'Day in The Life' by the Beatles.

"You are alive?" I ask.

"Yes, I've been with you the whole time," says Lennon. "All the voices you have been hearing have gotten you to where you are. In the end, I'm responsible for the whole thing."

I start to tear up.

"You're really alive?" I say. "Yes," says Lennon.

"You are not meant to be a reporter," says Lennon. "You are very musical. You're meant to be a rock musician. All you need to do is pick up a guitar and play, and you will become a famous celebrity."

"You mean like Don?" I ask.

"Yes, Don and Jane already knew that you were a rock musician. They gave you the idea to just be creative. You are born with amazing creativity. You are a born rock musician."

I am amazed.

All I need, according to Lennon, is a guitar.

Chapter 37

THE GUITAR

I sit on my bed, still amazed at the voice I am hearing.

"There is a music store close by to you," says Lennon. "Go ahead and buy a guitar from there. You also have a tape recorder. You can record your songs on there."

I wonder what it will be like to play the guitar. I have never played one before. But if I can play the violin and the piano, I should be able to play the guitar just as easily, I figure. However, when it comes to classical music, I was taught to play, whereas with the guitar I have never even touched it before.

Knowing my parents are in the house, I am careful to whisper to Lennon.

"I'll go get a guitar," I say.

"Good, go ahead and do that, and we can get started." I go to the kitchen where my mother is making lunch. "Hi Mum," I say.

"Hello, Gaddy."

"I was wondering about something. I am interested maybe in learning the guitar. Could I buy a guitar from the music store nearby?"

My mother pauses before answering. "A guitar?" she asks.

"Yeah, I thought it would be neat if I tried to learn the instrument."

"Do you need to take lessons?" she asks. "No, not really," I say.

"I guess it's okay," she says. "Go ahead." "Thanks Mom," I say.

After we eat lunch, I drive to the music store in Winfield. It is a very small store, but it has a good selection of guitars.

The man who works there has glasses, a big mustache and is balding.

"You want this one?" he asks pointing to one of the acoustic guitars.

"Yeah, that would be fine," I say.

I purchase the guitar and take it home.

I find my tape recorder in the basement. I then go to Walmart and buy some cassettes I can record on. I am very excited to see what I can do.

I come home, go to my room and shut the door. I strum the guitar. I have no idea how to tune it.

"Rock musicians don't worry about tuning," says Lennon. "Just play, and see what happens."

Lennon begins to tell me the truth about rock music.

"What happens is a rock musician records the music. He doesn't actually play on stage though. The performers on stage are not real but are hologram versions of the rock musicians. The hologram versions of the rock musicians also look different from the actual rock musicians themselves because if they didn't, the creators would get no privacy.

"So, you don't have to memorize anything, and you won't get chased around. You were born to create. When you have created the music, send it to a recording company, and they will create a hologram version of you to play your music on stage."

"Amazing," I say.

I create some tunes. However, I don't think anybody will actually like the music I am creating. It doesn't sound like rock music. It sounds way to atonal; I think.

"It doesn't matter what you create. The way your music becomes accepted is by you, taking risks. When you take lots of risks, with your type of soul, a creative soul, what you create automatically becomes famous."

I think, could this possibly be true?

I think about it for a while. The voice sounds so real and true. "The way to know if I am telling the truth," says Lennon, "is to listen to whether there is a ring of truth when I say something. As long as you can feel that, then you know that I am telling the truth." I listen to what Lennon says and it really sounds truthful.

After playing for a while, and talking to Lennon, I come out of my room.

My mum and dad are sitting at the dinner table. "I heard you playing in there," says my mum.

"Yeah, I've been experimenting with my guitar and my voice.

That's what real rock musicians do," I say.

"You want to be a rock musician?" asks my dad.

"Yes, I am a born rock musician and I am born very creative. I can create some of the greatest rock music ever."

"Don't you need to take lessons?" asks my mum again.

"No, I can play without lessons. I just need to pick up the guitar and play."

I realize that my parents are not saying anything against what I am doing because they are fearing that I might run out on them again.

After eating, I go back to my room. I listen to what I have created. "You're a genius," says Lennon.

I begin to think that my music is maybe more creative and experimental than that of anyone else.

"I am your guru," says Lennon. "The term guru is truly about the relationship between two entertainers."

Lennon also says he actually looks different from the hologram who appears on stage and in public.

"Why did you fake your assassination?" I ask.

"The hologram was drawing too many crowds, so we decided to do the assassination."

I play for a little while longer, and then get some sleep.

Chapter 38

RISKS

I wake up in the morning.

Suddenly, I hear the voice of Lennon again.

"You have taken your first big risk, which was to purchase a guitar and play," he says. "You need to take some more risks. You need to live more dangerously to become a famous celebrity."

I ask Lennon what I should do.

"Be completely fearless," he says. "Go crazy."

My parents are going on a trip to Gulf Shores, Alabama, for a few days, staying in a condo they own there.

Before they leave, my mum expresses concern about me staying by myself.

"Are you sure you are okay?" she asks. "Yeah, I will be fine," I say.

"Okay, if you need to call us, you can reach us at the Gulf Shores number."

I see my parents leave.

I then spend some more time, playing the guitar and recording my music. Again, I realize that because my music sounds so weird, I must be a very experimental rock musician.

I then go outside.

Our dog, Maggie, is sitting on the lawn. All of a sudden, I hear another voice.

"Hello Gaddy," says the voice. It is high pitched and sounds female.

The dog looks at me curiously. I stare at her for a while, not sure where the voice is coming from.

"Hello, it's the dog talking to you," says the voice. "Maggie?" I say.

"Yes, it's me," says Maggie.

"You have an amazing soul," she says. "You can even communicate with animals. Your soul is considered to be a very empathetic, peaceful soul."

I'm astonished.

"Don't be alarmed at all," says Maggie. "You really can communicate with us animals."

Suddenly, the voice of Lennon appears again.

"So, you know you can communicate with animals as well?" says Lennon.

"Yes," I say in amazement.

I begin to marvel at what a beautiful world this really is. This world is full of pleasant surprises that I had never known before. Life feels like so much more fun like this.

"You need to start taking some risks," says Maggie. There is a pool in our backyard.

I go inside the house and change into my bathing suit. I then come back out.

I go near the shallow end of the pool. "Go for it!" cries Lennon.

I jump into the pool at the shallow end. Luckily, I am not injured.

After doing that, Lennon tells me to take the ultimate risk. He tells me to stare directly into the sun.

"Nothing can harm you," says Lennon, "take any risk you like."

I then stare directly into the sun for a few minutes. Again, nothing bad happens. I begin to feel invincible. I realize I can do anything, and nothing can harm me.

"Wow, this is amazing," I say.

I then go outside to my car. I get in and start driving.

I drive all the way to Tuscaloosa.

While I am there, I go to one of the shopping malls. There is a movie theatre there. There are not that many people in the afternoon. I go inside and watch a movie — Men in Black.

I get bored with the movie and leave before it finishes. I eat lots of pizza and ice cream there as well.

"Eat for pleasure, not health," says Lennon. "If you eat for pleasure, you will end up being much healthier. You have been told a lot of lies. You are meant to gradually discover the truth by taking risks."

I then get into my car.

I drive back to Winfield.

I take another risk, driving my car very fast. There are not too many drivers on the road. I get home.

I feel very tired.

I then rest for a few hours.

Later, when it is night, I get up and start playing the guitar. I play for a few hours until I feel very tired.

I then go to sleep. My mother calls the next morning. I tell her I am doing fine.

"Are you sure you are okay?" she asks. "Yes," I say, "never felt better."

I then decide to do something crazier. I take off all my clothes and walk around the house.

I then walk outside and jump into the pool again. I feel so free of all my worries. Life is amazing. I feel like the luckiest man in the world.

Chapter 39

ROCK MUSIC

The next day, I wake up in the morning and eat ice cream for breakfast.

Soon after, I hear Lennon again.

"Way to go with taking those risks," he said. "You are very brave and fearless. The more risks you take, the more famous you become."

I pick up my guitar and start strumming again.

I create several songs before putting the guitar away.

I then listen to the songs on the tape recorder. My singing voice is very nasal sounding. I wonder how honestly people can like this music. But Lennon reassures me that the music will grow in popularity as I take more risks.

There is a video store close by to where we live. "Rent Rebel Without A Cause," says Lennon "You are very much like James Dean," he says. "James Dean was a real risk-taker."

Suddenly I hear another voice.

"Hi Gaddy — it's James Dean," the voice says. "I'm still alive as well."

Lennon says a lot of celebrities who appeared to have died are still alive.

"When it comes to actors," says Dean, "they don't have holographic images. What you see on screen is the actual person.

So quite a few actors have faked their deaths. We also undergo a surgical procedure to change our appearance when we don't want to be seen in public anymore."

"Amazing," I say.

"Take more risks. Be as rebellious as you can. That's the whole point of Rebel Without Cause — it's all about taking risks and being as brave as you can be."

"The music I have created, and the movies James was in are really meant specifically for you," adds Lennon. "The whole point of it is to encourage you to take risks so you will become a famous creator and celebrity in our world."

I then roam outside the house.

Lennon then says, "The greatest risk you can take is going to jail. If you take this risk, your celebrity status will increase by 200 percent."

I marvel at the thought of this.

The way, I figure, I can end up in jail is to take all my clothes off in a public place. I decide to go to a gas station and a McDonalds and take my clothes off there.

I get in my car and drive to a gas station.

I then go to the back of the gas station. While back there, I slowly remove all my clothes. I then approach the woman who is working at the gas station.

She has grey curly hair and glasses.

She sees me, looking at me with surprise in her eyes. "Put your clothes on!" she yells.

While I am in front of her, I slowly put my clothes back on. I feel elated.

What a risk to take. This has got to be the ultimate risk. I am so proud of myself for completely losing the fear to do this.

I then leave the gas station and go to McDonald's. There are very few customers there.

I then stand in front of the employees, mostly women, and I take my clothes off. The women stare at me astonished, not sure what to think. Somebody then contacts the police.

The police arrive at McDonald's.

They arrest me and take me to a jail in Hamilton, Alabama. I am cuffed.

I am wearing a tank top and jeans.

Having my hands in handcuffs is very painful. I can hardly maneuver around. It is very difficult to get in and out of the police car.

When we arrive in Hamilton, I am escorted into the jail. After waiting for a few moments for them to process me, I am led to a jail cell.

I am asked to remove my clothes, and wear a prison uniform. I am still feeling on top of the world, amazed at my bravery and my fearlessness. However, for a second, I am worried that the other inmates may be very violent and hostile towards me.

I am the only brown-skinned person there. Most of the other inmates are white, and there are a few black inmates.

I think the white inmates might be very racist and may want to harm me. So, while I am in jail, I take another risk and act completely crazy. I jump up and down and make noises like an ape.

It seems to work.

Nobody seems to be coming to get me. "Well done," says Lennon.

"No problem," I say.

While in jail, they serve me dinner.

Despite it being jail food, I feel rather hungry, and am quite content to eat the food.

The very small jail cell has a small toilet in it and metal bars. There is also a bed made of metal to sleep on. It is very uncomfortable. However, I am so happy to be taking risks and being fearless that I don't worry about where I am at all.

Chapter 40

JAIL

I sit quietly in the jail cell trying to meditate.

I figure what I am doing must be like meditation. I sit in a small place, with no entertainment for hours, only hearing my own thoughts echo through my head.

Again, Lennon speaks.

"Gaddy, you have a meditative soul," says Lennon. "You can spend hours with no entertainment, just sitting by yourself, listening to the Higher Power."

"The Higher Power communicates with me?" I ask.

"Yes, when you are in silence, the Higher Power is communicating with you," says Lennon.

One of the guards then brings me some breakfast.

As I eat, I sit and wonder if I will ever get out of here. I wonder also if my parents have found out that I am in jail. I figure they are worried. But I am not that concerned because I have a job to do, which is to create pleasure for the world.

"You are a C.O.P.," says Lennon.

"It stands for creator of pleasure. You have the most important job on earth, which is to create pleasure for others."

"I guess that is my duty," I say.

"Yes. We all have a duty on earth or a purpose in life," says Lennon.

It is then, I hear some footsteps coming toward my jail cell.

The guard, a burly man with a mustache, opens the jail cell.

"Your parents are here," he says. "Ah, thank you," I respond.

I get out of the jail cell. The guard tells me to remove my jumpsuit and get dressed. All I have is a tank top, some underwear and some jeans, clothes I wore when I took the risks that got me here.

I get dressed and go to the main entrance of the jail. I see my parents standing there.

My mother has such a sad expression on her face. When she sees me, she starts crying? It is unbearable to watch her cry like this, but still, I have a job to do, a job the Higher Power wants me to do.

My dad, meanwhile, stares nervously at me, while also looking at the floor.

My dad and mother then thank one of the jail workers for keeping me safe.

"We'll be going to the psychiatric ward in Tuscaloosa," my dad says to me.

"Do you have all your things?" he asks "Yes, I do," I say.

The three of us get into my dad's car. We then drive to Tuscaloosa. My parents are very silent the whole way. We say nothing to each other.

I then begin to hear other voices.

"He's a mental patient," says one voice. "He's such a loser." "Rich and spoiled is what he is," says another voice.

The voice of Lennon seems to have disappeared temporarily. "Has no job," says a voice "And he's all alone — has no friends."

I have learned not to respond to the voices when in public.

Instead, I say something with my mind, calling the voices a bunch of jerks.

We finally arrive at the psychiatric ward. My parents escort me inside.

There is a nurse to greet us.

She is skinny with brown hair and wearing glasses. "We'll take of care of him," says the nurse to my parents. "Thank you," my mother says.

My mother and father then hug me. Despite feeling angry, they still seem to care about me and hope that I will feel better. It's unfortunate that this is happening, but I have no choice — I have to go through with this.

Like my last visit, I again go back into the main room where there are lots of mental patients. I spend most of my time there.

Lennon suddenly reappears.

"You're such a risk-taker. Ending up here is another risk you have taken to help the world," he says. "You're a creative genius, a creator of pleasure."

I see other patients talking to themselves.

"What about them?" I ask Lennon. "Are they, creators of pleasure?"

"No," says Lennon. "Most of the human beings you see on earth are part of the hologram. They are not real. There are only a few hundred people who are real, who exist on earth," he says.

"The hologram is what guides a real human being on their journey to discovering themselves," says Lennon. "They do this by sending subliminal messages to real human beings. They do this both verbally and non-verbally."

"Are there more creative souls?" I ask.

"Yes, there are, and they are all going through the same thing you are going through. They are all creators of pleasure, including writers, actors, and rock musicians."

"So, the celebrities are all creative souls?" I ask. "Yes," says Lennon.

"And they are human beings — not just part of the hologram?" I ask.

"Yes — celebrities and creative souls are real, while all the other human beings are just part of the hologram."

"Why didn't I know this, to begin with?" I ask.

"To figure out the truth about the hologram, you again need to take plenty of risks. When you take more risks, more truth is revealed to you."

"I see," I say.

Suddenly, Lennon's voice disappears again, and I start hearing other voices again.

"What a lazy, good for nothing he is," says a voice. "He is so lucky to have parents like he has."

I then leave the main room in the ward and go back to bed.

I soon fall asleep, amazed at how important I must be to this world.

Chapter 41

ADULT CHILD

After a few weeks, I am released from the psychiatric ward.

My parents come to pick me up.

I really want to get out of here. This place is so boring and depressing. The food is okay but not great. I tell the psychiatrist that I am feeling fine, whenever he asks me. Even though I am still hearing things, I really want the psychiatrist to release me from here.

The other thing is we eat meals, but we don' t get any snacks. I feel very hungry in between meals.

My parents greet me, each of them hugging me. "How are you?" asks my mother.

"Fine," I say.

Despite previously enjoying taking risks, I am not feeling happy about being in the psychiatric ward. This risk led to more pain rather than pleasure. I would rather do anything I can to stay out of here. Being in the psychiatric ward deters me from taking more risks.

While I am driving home, I start to hear voices other than Lennon.

"He's such a loser," a voice says. "He's going home to live with his parents. He's nothing but an adult child."

After about an hour, we arrive in Winfield. I get out of the car.

Maggie, the dog, is there to greet me. I pet her and kiss her fur.

I am very happy to see her again.

"How are you?" she says.

My parents are there, but only I can hear her.

I communicate with her through my mind rather than through talking.

"I'm doing great," I say to her.

"Well done with all those risks," she says. "You are an amazing soul."

"Thank you," I say.

My parents and I enter the house. The house is very isolated. There is a lot of farmland surrounding the house. Our closest neighbors live a fair distance away from us. When I took risks, around my house, the neighbors couldn't see me.

I am so happy to be home.

I am very hungry, and I immediately raid the refrigerator. I grab some bread from the fridge and also help myself to some ice cream. I really enjoy my snack. I feel so happy just to be alive for a little while.

Then I hear voices again.

"What's he going to do here?" asks a voice. "Just waste his time all day."

"His dad is a rich doctor. He is nothing but a rich doctor's son." "They should just kick him out of the house," another voice says. "He really deserves it."

To please the voices, I do very wholesome activities. I sit in one of the rooms in the house, which has lots of books on a bookshelf. I decide to sit and read all day. I want to show that I'm not spoiled - that I am a good person.

I help my mother out with the dishes as well.

During the evenings, I go outside the house, and walk on the grass. While I am out there, I talk to Maggie with my mind.

"Are you going to take more risks?" she asks.

"No," I say. "I don't want to end up back at the institution again."

"That's probably best," she says.

"I really don't want to end up in jail again either," I say. As night falls, I take my medication.

I take Zyprexa. I am afraid to not take my medication because if I don't, I could end up back in the psychiatric ward again. At first, when I took the medicine, I was afraid it could harm me. I really didn't want to take it. But, after a while, I realized I had no choice. Besides reading, I also rent movies from a video store close by.

My parents and I watch movies at night.

All seems well, but I continue to hear voices scolding me for the way I am living.

"He's so spoiled," says a voice.

One day, I pick up the newspaper, and there is an article, an opinion piece, on adult children living with their parents. The article says that adults who live with their parents are spoiled rotten, and should be forced to go to work and fend for themselves.

"Don't spoil your kids," the article says, "otherwise, they will never leave. Make them earn what they get from you."

Not only are there articles in the newspaper on this, but there are also television talk shows, which talk about this as well.

One show says that kids who live with their parents never learn how to be independent. The talk show host says that when kids are spoiled, they learn to rely on others for help all the time rather than helping themselves.

I also see lots of stuff on the Internet about adult children as well.

Only one article, out of many, says that children living with their parents is okay. If the parents don' t mind it, then there is nothing wrong with it, says the article.

I try to do good things, like reading and helping my mother with the dishes.

None of the stuff I see, says anything about adult children who have a mental illness. I figure there must be other young adults, like me, who are going through the same thing. However, there is hardly anything written by adult children or parents who support the idea of their kids living at home.

I wish I could communicate with others who have the same problems that I am having. Though I enjoy solitude, this makes me feel kind of alone.

Chapter 42

OAKVILLE

After one more year in Winfield, my parents and I decide to move back to Canada. My sister lives in Toronto and has two younger children. My parents want to be closer to them.

My dad, after looking for a job in several different locations, finally accepts a job in Oakville, Ontario.

Oakville's population is mainly Caucasian. Other places close to Toronto, like Mississauga or Brampton, have more Indians and Indo-Canadians living there.

Toronto itself is also extremely multi-cultural. I have never lived in a place where my race is so prevalent. Every place I have lived in before is mainly Caucasian. Despite that, I still hear mainly Caucasian voices saying that I am spoiled rotten.

However, a lot of Indo-Canadians, and Indians, who are my age, still live with their parents. In India, most families never separate from each other. There may be two or three generations living under the same roof.

I wonder why Caucasians, and other races, are not the same way as Indians. Isn't it much easier to live under one roof, where you have all your family there to support you? You end up feeling less alone, and there is always somebody to help you out, especially when you need someone to take care of your kids.

Since there are more Indians around, as well, I feel like I don't stand out as much anymore. I feel like I am just one of the crowd, rather than feeling that I am the only Indian person on the street.

The house we live in is a fairly big house with extra bedrooms, in case my parents have company. We have a lot of relatives who live close by to Oakville and Toronto so, in general, we feel less alone.

My sister, my brother-in-law and their two children come over to visit us every weekend.

The two children are very young, and are a lot of fun to hang out with.

While in Oakville, I feel better and decide to start looking for a job. Oakville has two main newspapers. I phone both, and send them my resume. I also send them clippings of the work I did while I was in Selma.

I figure since my work was well-liked in Selma; I would easily land a job in Oakville. However, after waiting a few weeks, and then a few months, I still haven't landed a job.

Despite this, I hear that there is an orchestra in Oakville. The orchestra is mainly made up of volunteers. I dig out my violin again and start practicing. At first, it feels somewhat frustrating because I haven' t played in such a long time.

I then, show up for orchestra practice. I am easily accepted into the orchestra. The orchestra needs a few more second violins, so I decided to play second violin.

My parents also buy a piano while we are in Oakville.

I start practicing on the piano again as well, again gradually easing into it.

After a few months, and after my playing has improved, I decide that I may want to teach violin and piano. There are a few music schools around in the area. I apply for a few jobs, and get accepted at one of the music schools in Oakville, called Michael's Music Store.

The owners of the store, who are married, are both very good pianists. They are both from the former Yugoslavia. He is a tall man who wears glasses, while she is a very attractive woman with long brown hair. They are both very kind. I consider myself lucky to have such good bosses.

While I am playing in the orchestra, I still hear voices.

The orchestra is made up of amateurs and professionals. Sometimes, I hear the voices of professionals criticizing my playing, calling me a mere amateur.

"He's not really that good," says a voice.

"He really needs to find another job. He should stick to being a journalist rather than trying to have a career in music."

While in the orchestra, I also decide to try and create my own quartet. I ask some of the amateurs in the orchestra if they would like to play in my quartet.

Amazingly enough, one of the men I ask, named Horace, happens to also have schizophrenia as well. He is about my height and has blonde hair.

"Yeah, I would be interested," he says, smiling. The other people I ask echo the same sentiment.

Horace lives in Toronto and commutes to Oakville to play in the orchestra.

He says he goes to see his psychiatrist at the Centre for mental health and addiction in Toronto better known as CAMH.

I am feeling better and I have stopped taking my medicine.

It's really interesting to have two people, who play music, both having the same kind of mental illness. Playing in the quartet is a lot of fun as well. We play a lot of Mozart, some Beethoven as well as other composers.

I really enjoy just playing again.

I also watch a lot of famous violinists on YouTube. I watch violinists like Itzhak Perlman and Jascha Heifetz. I try to pick up on things that they are doing in order to improve my own playing.

I try to practice a few hours a day.

I also do yoga to improve my posture while playing. Yehudi Menuhin, a famous violinist, was known for doing yoga after he was injured in order to improve his playing. Menuhin, I think, is so amazing. When he plays, he has such a presence. You can't take your eyes off him.

Despite all of this, I still continue to hear voices. "He's still living with his parents," says a voice.

"When it comes to music, he won't make much money since he is an amateur."

I also take lessons from the concertmaster of the Oakville Symphony. He is a tall man with grey, curly hair. He is quite hard, on me. He says that the most important thing in about playing the violin is to have good posture and be very relaxed.

He says yoga will really help with this.

"You need to be loose," he says. "You need to let go."

Despite him telling me this, I still am not able to do what he wants. In general, I play only one scale with him and one study. I think we are getting nowhere. I wish I could do what he wants and improve, but eventually, I decide this is going nowhere so I decide to quit taking lessons.

I play in concerts once a month. Just hearing and playing classical music is such a pleasure — it keeps me going in spite of the voices I am hearing.

For now, everything seems to be going well.

Chapter 43

LIES

Suddenly, I hear Lennon's voice again. "How are you, Gaddy?" he asks.

"I'm fine," I say. "You're back again."

"Yes," says Lennon. "I'm still here. I never went away." He pauses.

He then adds, "There are many things you need to know about this world. Most of what you believe in is a lie."

"What do you mean?" I ask.

"For example, there is no outer space," says Lennon. "Nobody has ever travelled into space. What you see on television and read in books is a bunch of nonsense."

"As for the news," he says, "it's all a bunch of lies. Everything you see is part of the hologram. Real people mainly live in cities like Toronto and Los Angeles. Everything else you see is nothing but the hologram."

"The only thing is you can't say anything about this," he says. "If you do, they will put you in an institution."

"There are other creative souls who are making the same discoveries that you are making. They all have different gurus like me. As for the world wars, and other wars as well, it is all fiction. It is more lies told by the hologram. As for the automobile. it is has always existed its present form."

"How many real people are there?" I ask.

"There are about 100," says Lennon. "Everybody else is just part of the hologram."

I am amazed.

I still have a tape of the rock music I have created. Lennon tells me to send the tape to a recording company.

"Go ahead and send it," says Lennon. "Your music will become very famous."

I look for a recording company on one of my cassettes. I decide to go with EMI.

I put the tape in an envelope and tell them who I am. I then drive to the post office, and mail the tape to the recording company.

After I come home, I see my mother in the kitchen. "Lunch is almost ready," she says.

"Thanks," I say.

Lennon tells me that my parents are also part of the hologram. "Everybody in the hologram sends you subliminal messages so you will end up in the right place doing what you are supposed to do on this earth," he says.

"Life is really this weird?" I ask. "Yes," says Lennon. "this weird."

I become enraptured in my conversations with Lennon. Soon, I begin to want to talk to Lennon all day, and learn the truth about life on earth. I want to be with him so much that I want to quit being in the orchestra and quit teaching music.

I am so distracted by Lennon that I tell my parents that I need to quit.

"Why?" asks my dad.

"I just don't feel like doing this anymore," I say.

"You are doing so well — why do you want to quit?" he asks. "I just don't feel like doing it anymore," I say again.

I phone the orchestra manager and tell her I am quitting.

I then, phone the music store and tell the owners, I am quitting. The male owner of the store asks me why I want to quit.

I tell him that I have other things I want to do. He sounds very displeased and very unhappy with my decision.

"You really should think about it," he says.

"I can't do it anymore," I say. "Please reconsider," he says.

"I can't, that's all I can tell you," I say.

I then, put down the phone. I feel horrible about having to quit my job, but at the same time, I realize I have more important things to do on planet earth.

After a few weeks, I receive a letter from EMI.

It says they have listened to the music, but that they have decided not to accept my recording. I stare in bewilderment at the letter. Lennon promised me that my music would be accepted.

"Don't worry about it," says Lennon. "You will eventually be accepted. Just keep sending your tape everywhere you can."

"Are you lying to me?" I ask Lennon. "No Gaddy, I swear I am not."

I begin to wonder about everything I have been told by Lennon. Maybe I am just hearing voices that are telling me things that are not true.

But the problem is the voice sounds so real. It's hard not to be convinced.

My parents talk to me about seeing another psychiatrist.

"I am fine," I say defiantly. "I don't need to see another psychiatrist."

"You're not fine," says my dad.

"You are doing all sorts of crazy things with your life. You really need to go see someone," he says.

"I won't go," I say.

"You won't make me go."

I get up from the dinner table and go to my room, slamming the door.

I lie on my bed.

"Are you alright?" asks Lennon. "Yeah, I'm fine," I say.

"Keep doing what I am telling you to do. I am your guru. Keep listening to me. You need to fulfill your purpose on earth."

"Okay," I say

I continue talking to Lennon, whispering in my room to him, hoping my parents won't hear me talking to myself.

Life is has become very confusing again. I can only hope things will get better.

Chapter 44

TIM

While I am lying in bed, I start to hear another familiar voice.

It is the voice of Tim, my friend from Prince George. "Hey, Gaddy?"

"Tim?" I ask in amazement. "Yeah, it's me," he says.

"How are you communicating with me?" I ask.

"We can communicate through our minds, whenever we feel like it. It is all done through the hologram."

"You are part of the hologram?" I ask. "Yes," he says.

"We were meant to meet back then. I know Lennon very well. He has been communicating with me the entire time to get you to the right place."

"Amazing," I say.

"I knew you were meant to become a famous rock musician. We tried to send subliminal messages to you the entire way to communicate to you that you were meant to be a celebrity rock musician."

I suddenly start to tear up. I miss Tim.

"I miss hanging out with you," I say.

"Yeah, we had some fun times together," he says.

"I remember how we were around women. We never could seem to get anywhere."

"Women liked you back then," says Tim. "They really did."
"Even without working out?" I ask.

"Yes. But all of us tried to send subliminal messages to you to get you to workout. This is just something you are meant to do as a celebrity."

"I remember when we hung out together," I say, "especially in Vancouver. I was totally lost in Vancouver. You showed me around the entire city. Even though we got nowhere with women, and we got poor marks, I really enjoyed hanging out with you."

"Yeah, I had fun too Gaddy."

"Life was much simpler than," I say. "I wasn't by myself all the time like I am now. I like being in solitude, but sometimes I miss hanging out with you."

"It was fun," he says, "but you were meant to do greater things." I then hear a knock on my bedroom door.

It is my mother.

"Are you alright?" she asks. "Yeah, I'm fine," I say.

"Dinner is ready. Do come upstairs and eat." My parents and I sit at the table.

My mother asks, "Are you sure you don't want to join the orchestra again?"

"No, I don't," I say. "I am meant to do other things." "Such as?" my father asks.

"I am meant to be a famous rock musician. I just know I am."

Life starts to become really weird because I realize my parents are part of the hologram and are trying to communicate subliminally to tell me what I am meant to do.

If I tell them I am hearing voices, though, I will be taken back to the institution.

It is like playing some weird game. Suddenly, I hear Lennon's voice again. "You will be fine," he says.

Then I hear Lennon start to laugh.

The laugh sounds so out of place, and funny, that I begin to smile and laugh right in front of my parents.

"Why are you smiling?" asks my mother.

Unsure of what exactly to say, I reply, "I'm just smiling, what's wrong with that?"

"There is nothing funny going on," says my dad. "Why are you laughing?"

I hear Lennon laugh again.

Again, I start to smile and then laugh. My parents look very concerned.

"Stop doing that," says my mother. "I'm sorry, I can't help it," I say.

I then communicate with Lennon through my mind and tell him to stop laughing.

"You'll be fine," says Lennon. "Don't worry — you are just meant to go through this."

"You really need to see a psychiatrist," says my mother. "I'm fine," I say. "I don't need to go see a shrink."

I then get up from the dinner table and go to my room. "You will be fine," says Lennon.

"Don't worry," says Tim, "everything will be okay." "I don't want to end up back at the institution," I say.

"You need to be prepared for anything," says Lennon. "Whatever the Higher Power wants you to do, you need to do it, even it means going back to the institution."

"Okay, I guess," I say, accepting my fate. I then ask Lennon a question.

"It's all up to the Higher Power?"

"Yes, everything that you are meant to do must be done through the Higher Power. Whatever happens to you, the Higher Power is behind it. So just know everything will be fine, and the Higher Power is always with you."

"I guess that makes sense," I say. "Yes," says Lennon, "you will be fine."

Chapter 45

RUNYON

I wake up the next morning.

I go upstairs to the kitchen and eat breakfast. I still eat a lot of sugar because I think sugar will not harm me.

I decide to work out at a gym nearby in the morning.

I realize that the hologram wants me to work out, as much as possible, and be a good-looking celebrity.

When I get home, I go to my room expecting to hear from Lennon.

"Hi Gaddy," he says. "Hi," I say.

"There is something else I need to tell you. You might have figured out that I didn't fake my assassination because I was too popular, — it was just something that was meant to happen in the hologram.

"The assassination was also meant to get you to be more interested in my music and that you would eventually figure out that I was your guru. I know when you read or heard about my assassination you became very saddened and wished that I was still alive."

"Yes, you are my hero," I say. "I am so overjoyed to know that you are still around."

"Thanks, Gaddy."

I pace up and down in my room all day, listening to the voices.

I rarely ever leave my room.

Lennon still tells me to take risks, however.

Sometimes, I go shopping and while I am driving there, I drive my car very fast. I also lift a tremendous amount of weight at the gym, and I never get injured. I also wear a tank top sometimes to show off my body.

While I am lying in my room, I hear another familiar voice. "Hi Gaddy, do you remember me?"

"Who is it?" I ask.

"It's me, Runyon — the kid who bullied you." "Runyon?"

"Yeah. I know John as well," he says. "I was supposed to bully you in order to make you a cooler person. You did everything we expected you would do. We, especially, wanted to get you into working out so that you would be more attractive to women."

"I can't believe you did that," I say.

Every day after I bullied you, I would come home and cry tears. I felt so bad about making your life so miserable. You were a nice kid — it was really tough to bully somebody who was so nice. "I am not what I appear to be," he says. "I am very into academics. I really love reading a lot. I am way more into my brain than I appeared to be."

"Yeah, I remember you failed a grade," I say.

" I was just pretending," he says. "As for all the other kids, who made fun of you, they're all the same way."

"After the class was over," he says, "we would all gather at a house nearby and talk to John everyday every day. John would instruct us about what to do in order to bully you and make you into a cool celebrity.

"I kept telling John that I was afraid that I might really hurt you. John, however, knew you very well, and knew for sure that you would be fine."

It is then I hear Lennon again.

"I have known about you since you were a small child," says Lennon. "I have been communicating with you the whole time.

"There is something else you need to know. All the stars in the sky belong to creative souls or real human beings. Every real human being is born inside a certain star. When a woman gets pregnant, the star of her child beams on her, and then, the child is eventually born.

"This is what immaculate conception really means," he says. "Every real human being, or creative soul, also has a guru. I have been communicating with you through the stars forever. After communicating with you through the stars, I then, meet you on earth, and I become your guru — while you are my disciple.

"As for you Gaddy, you will have a disciple as well, and you will do the same things for your disciple as I have done for you."

I am amazed at how the universe really works.

"The stars are very important," says Lennon. "All our communication occurs through the stars."

I hear Runyon again.

"You are a very good person," he says. "Despite all the crazy things you have done, you have done them because the Higher Power wanted you to do them. The definition of a good person is not quite what you thought it was."

"I agree with that," I say. It is then, I hear Tim again. "Hey Gaddy," he says.

"I knew Runyon as well when you were being bullied," he says. "When you got to our high school, you were already on your way to being a cooler person because of Runyon. That is when I met you, and then, sent you subliminal messages in order to get you to the right place."

"So, it was all acting?" I say.

"Yes," said Lennon. "The hologram did a very good job. You are a cool celebrity. By being like this, you will create pleasure in our world — which is very important to the world."

It is then, I hear a knock on the door. "Dinner,' says my mum again.

Chapter 46

TORONTO

A few days later, Lennon asks me to do something different. "Gaddy, you would be way better living on your own," he says. "Are you sure?" I ask.

"Yes. When you are by yourself, you can live more freely. You also don't have to be so careful around your parents, especially when you are talking to me."

"Should I ask them for my own place?" "Yes," says Lennon.

"I'll go ahead and do it," I say.

I leave my room and walk upstairs to the kitchen. My mother is by herself in the kitchen, making a snack for herself.

"Mom," I say.

"Yes, Gaddy."

"I think I would be better living on my own," I say. "You want to live by yourself?"

"Yes. I really would lead a much better life if I were more independent of you. All three of us living together is cramping my style."

"Are you sure you're okay?" she asks.

"Yes, I am fine," I say. "I need to take more risks with my life, and challenge myself way more."

"Okay, 'I'll talk to your dad about it when he gets home," she says. I am very glad she is considering it.

A few hours later, my dad comes back from work.

I am in my room.

My mother comes downstairs and knocks at my bedroom door. "Dinner is ready," she says.

I go upstairs and sit at the kitchen table. "So, you want to move out?" asks my dad.

"Yes. I think it's about time I did. I don't want to be such a burden on both of you."

"We think it is a good idea," says my mother. "We can purchase a condo in Toronto for you. It might be better for you if you lived on your own. I agree with you, Gaddy. The more independent you are the better off you are."

"I'm glad you agree," I say.

"We will look for a new place for you," says my dad.

A few days later, my mother tells me that she and my dad have found a condo I can live in.

"It's right in downtown Toronto," says my mum excitedly. "It's a very nice place. Everything is right there. There is also a grocery store exactly in the same building as well."

The condo is called Maple Leaf Square. It is right near the Air Canada Centre where professional sports teams play in Toronto.

My parents and I drive over to the condo.

"The subway is close by as well," says my mother. "You don't even need a car to get around."

The condo looks very nice.

My mum and dad purchase some furniture for the condo.

The condo is quite expensive, costing hundreds of thousands of dollars, but my parents have enough money to buy it.

I am very grateful.

"Thanks for helping me out," I say. "No problem," says my father.

"You can live more independently this way, and we won't be in each other's crosshairs all the time," says my mother. "I think having your own place is a very good idea. You have to rely more on yourself and not as much on us. This will make both our lives better."

We then go back to Oakville. I pack my things.

I am so happy to be moving out. I can now communicate with Lennon, and the others, without having to worry about my parents overhearing me. I can also take more risks in order to become a famous celebrity as soon as possible.

My parents and I drive back to the condo, and my parents drop me off.

We give each other a quick hug and then my parents leave.

There are two bedrooms in the condo, as well as two bathrooms, in case I have company, mainly my parents, who may want to stay over.

I lie in a bed in one of the bedrooms and communicate with Lennon.

"You are finally free," says Lennon. "Yes," I say.

I then go into my kitchen, which is in the same room as the living room, and open the refrigerator.

I have nothing to eat.

I decided to take the elevator down and go to the grocery store. The grocery store is very nice, and has a good selection of stuff. It even has a sushi place.

I am still into eating a sugary diet.

I buy some boxes of ice cream and some hot dogs, which are very easy to make.

I decide to eat the ice cream for lunch and the hot dogs for dinner. I hardly need any food, I figure, I can survive on very little, and spend way less.

It is almost the same as it was when I was in Mississippi.

However, this time I have my parents blessing.

There is a television in the condo, but I watch it very rarely.

Most of the time is spent communicating with Lennon and the other voices. I walk around in the living room in circles and talk to Lennon, without having to whisper, all day.

Lennon then says not to take any bigger risks. "What you are doing now is fine Gaddy," he says. "You don't want me to go to jail again?" I ask.

"No. Just take it easy on the risk-taking, and keep leading the life you are leading. Things are going as they should," he says.

Chapter 47

BETRAYAL

I hear Lennon's voice the next morning. "How are you feeling Gaddy?" he asks. "Doing fine," I say.

"Know I will be with you always," says Lennon.

"I am so glad to know you're alive," I say. "Right now, I feel so happy."

I begin to wonder about my parents, and why they were not concerned about me living by myself. I figure out the reason. They thought because I showed signs of wanting to be independent that my disease must have disappeared.

I phone my mother and ask her about this.

"Yes," she says. "Your dad and I figured that if you were showing independence, you must be feeling better. So, we decided not to argue against you being on your own."

"Thanks mum, for helping me out," I say. "No problem," she says.

After that, I hear Lennon again.

"Your music will become very famous," he says.

"Do I need to send my tape to another recording company?" I ask.

"Don't worry about it," he says. "Everything will happen on its own. The hologram will take care of everything." "Are you okay?" asks Lennon.

"I'm fine," I say. "You're sure?" he asks.

"What do you mean?" I ask.

"Well, I just thought that you might be feeling lonely," he says. "You encouraged me to be alone," I say.

"Yes, I know."

After conversing for a bit, I then decide I need some more groceries.

I go to the store downstairs. I buy a couple of cartons of some ice cream as we all as some whipping cream. I also buy some buns and wieners to make hot dogs. It is then I hear Lennon laughing.

I get back to my condo. "What's so funny?" I ask.

"You're so alone," says Lennon. "You really should be hanging out with lots of friends and partying like crazy. You're still young."

"What?" I say.

"You're kind of nerdy," he says.

"John, what are you talking about?" I ask. I start to feel shivery.

"You need people in your life," says Lennon. "Without lots of people, your life ends up being very depressing and lonely."

"I thought you were all about living in solitude," I say. "I was. But I am not anymore."

I hear laughter again.

"Gaddy, I am not who you think I am." "What?"

"I am somebody else, and heavily dislike your friend John Lennon for being so liberal in his views."

I feel afraid.

"I am not Lennon. I am the United States government. We are still after you because you pose a threat to the United States by being so liberal."

I feel a choking sensation again.

This time, however, I become less afraid. I am now extremely angry, which makes my fear disappear.

"You fucking bastard," I say.

"You're a nice guy Gaddy, but you are far too liberal. You're a threat to the United States."

I start yelling at the voice.

I scream very loudly, and yell lots of profanity. A few hours later, I hear a knock on the door.

I open the door. Standing outside are two police officers. One has Chinese features, while the other is Caucasian. "What are you doing here?" I ask.

"The neighbors are complaining about the noise. You are behaving very violently. We have to arrest you."

In defiance, I try to shut the door, but one of the policemen sticks his foot in the doorway preventing me from closing it.

I scream very loudly.

The policeman then opens the door.

They put handcuffs on me and take me down to their police car.

After wrestling me into the police car, they drive me to CAMH, the center for addiction and mental health in Toronto.

I am now a mental patient once again.

Chapter 48

CAMH

I am escorted by the police onto one of the floors at CAMH. The police release me from my handcuffs and then leave.

There are a few psychiatric nurses to help me settle down here. One of the nurses is Chinese and speaks with a strong Chinese accent. She tells me to sit on one of the chairs, that are all lined up in the main sitting area.

She goes into an office and then comes back with some gowns for me to wear.

She then escorts me to the room where I will be staying. The room is very small and there is a window, which allows you to see into the room. I feel like I have absolutely no privacy here.

While I am in the room, I change clothes and put on my gowns. "You will see the psychiatrist tomorrow," she says. "Go ahead and get some sleep."

I thank her for her help and then lay on the bed. The bed feels a little stiff.

I can't believe I have ended up in the institution again. I then start to hear other voices.

"What a loser," a voice says.

"He looks rich and spoiled," says another voice. "His parents are probably helping me out big time. I wish I had parents like that."

These are the voices I hear of other patients who are staying there.

I try to sleep, but I find it quite difficult. I get up occasionally and pace in my small, little room. I hear footsteps coming down the hall. I figure there is a curfew, and I need to be in bed rather than pacing around.

Slowly and painfully, I fall asleep. I wake up the next morning. I get up early, and I leave my room. I see a nurse standing in the main patient area.

I feel very hungry.

"Is breakfast being served yet?" I ask.

"No, not for another three hours," says the nurse. "I feel kind of hungry," I say.

"You just have to wait until breakfast is served," says the nurse.

I thank the nurse and I go sit on one of the chairs. I feel like I am doing meditation. There is no television in the main sitting area. I sit and stare at the nurse and other patients walking past me.

Many of the patients wander around in circles talking to themselves. I wonder if any of the patients might be violent or racist. Despite thinking this, I am not afraid of anything anymore. After having gone through what I have gone through, I completely lose the fear of everything.

A nurse then comes over to me.

"The doctor is here to see you," she says. I go into a small office.

The doctor has grey hair and is wearing glasses. "Hi, my name is Dr. Gene Dixon," he says. "Gaddy Das," I say.

I shake his hand.

"What is the problem?" he asks. "I'm hearing voices,' I say.

"What do the voices tell you?" he asks.

"They tell me that I am a loser, that I am spoiled and that I rely on my parents too much,"

"Are you hearing them right now?" he asks. "Ah, it's not really that bad right now," I say.

"You will need to take some medicine," he says. "The medicine you will be taking is called clozapine."

I have taken medicine before, and nothing bad happened with the medicine, so I figure I might as well agree to take it again. I am also very fearless now, which helps as well.

"When you take clozapine, you will also need to get your blood work done. It's to make sure that your white blood cell count is not too low. This can be a side effect of the medicine."

"That's fine," I say.

"How long will I be staying here?" I ask. "Probably, another week or so," he says. "Thanks," I say.

"You can get your medicine at the counter over there," he says. "No problem."

"It was nice meeting you," he says, "I will talk to you later." "Thanks," I say.

I go to the counter and get my medicine,

The nurse hands me some pills. She tells me to open the package, they are in, and then gives me some water.

"It's good for you to get used to taking the medicine yourself," she says.

"No problem," I say.

I take the medicine and go sit back on one of the chairs. I then hear a nurse saying breakfast is served.

I am overwhelmed with happiness. I finally get to eat. I feel so hungry. I desperately want to get out of this place. This place, even though it may help patients, doesn't have the comforts of home. I feel I have no privacy here.

I especially hate the window that lets others look inside my room.

I stare at the bathroom as well. I am almost afraid to have a shower because the place is littered with wet towels. I also still wonder if anybody staying here is prone to violence.

Chapter 49

GETTING BETTER

After a few days, I begin to wonder how I can avoid ever coming back to this place again. I still hear voices occasionally, but I realize that I shouldn't react to them. The best thing to do, I figure, is to ignore them.

How do you not react to the voices?

I figure it is almost like meditation. You hear the voices and let it pass. Don't react to the voice. If you react to the voice in anger, you will end up in the institution again.

I begin to realize I can develop a philosophy or religion out of my disease. The philosophy or religion is all about being compassionate. Even if you hear a voice that disturbs you, or you hear somebody actually say something negative about you, instead of reacting angrily, be compassionate.

When you are compassionate to others, your life will really improve.

I sit in a chair in the main area.

I look at others who are talking to themselves and walking around in circles. I realize that my disease might not be as bad as others who are here. They may be hearing voices so much that they hardly have anytime any time to reflect on what is going on with them.

I begin to think I can possibly help these people.

With my insights into my own disease, I can advise psychiatrists and patients on how to handle schizoaffective disorder. I can also educate people about mental illness.

When you have a mental illness, this does not make you a bad or lazy person. People fail to understand this, and they wallow in ignorance. They say bad things about people with mental illness, like they are responsible for their illness or that they fail to socialize enough, which is what they think causes the disease.

Avoiding anger at any cost is the most important thing. Religions like Buddhism encourage you not to get angry. When you get angry, you lose control of yourself, which could eventually lead to violence.

The best thing to do is to stay calm and rational. Don't let what people say affect your behavior. Even if someone says something negative, if you stay calm, you end up winning in the end.

This, I now believe, all ties into wanting to be a good person. When you focus on being a good person, rather than worrying as much on being a success in life, your life will improve.

My mother constantly talks about being a good person. I realize I can learn so much from her about this, and that by listening to her, I can really improve my life.

I also have read books by people like the Dalai Lama. When you comprehend what the Dalai Lama is saying, and incorporate this into your life, your life will begin to improve.

While I am sitting in the chair, I see my parents arriving. I am so happy to see them. Life is boring at the institution, and I long to see somebody I know.

"Hey Gaddy," says my mother. "Hi," I say.

"How are you?"

"Doing okay," I say. "Let's go to my room and talk. We will have more privacy there."

We walk to my room.

"Are you doing okay?" asks my dad.

"Yes," I say, "I really am looking forward to getting out of here. I also am feeling much better. I realize now that I really have a disease. and that this is what is causing all my problems."

"It is very important you realize that," says my mother.

"The voices I am hearing I know are not real," I say. "I still hear them, a little, but I think I know how to deal with them now."

"Are you taking the medicine?" asks my dad.

"Yes, I am taking it every day," I say. "I think it may be helping with the disease."

"The psychiatrist said it is very important that you stay on the medicine and take the medicine every day. If you miss taking it, the disease will come back," my dad warns.

I feel very thirsty.

"Could you bring some regular Coke the next time you come?" I ask.

"Yes," says my mother. "Is that all you need?" "Yes, I think I have everything else," I say.

I then say, "The showers here are horrible. There are all sorts of wet towels all over the floor. I try to take a shower every second day, if I can.

"I also really miss being home," I say.

"There is no privacy here. The other thing I sometimes worry about is if any of the patients are violent."

"Don't worry," says my mother. "You will be fine."

"After having this disease, I am very fearless now," I say. "I'm sure you're right, everything will be okay."

"We have to get going," says my mother.

"Are you sure you don't need anything?" my dad asks. "I'm fine," I say.

"Take care Gaddy, we will see you soon," says my mother. My parents hug me and then leave.

I then stare at the clothes that I packed before I came here. I just brought a pouch bag. I have only one change of shirt, socks, and underwear.

I want to wash my clothes, but there are so many people doing laundry here.

I go and sit back in the chair.

The nurses bring out some coffee. I put some NutraSweet in my coffee, and begin to drink contentedly.

I then realize that I should start eating healthy again.

I have become less healthy because of these stupid voices. I also realize how delusional I was. I was thinking of all sorts of crazy things, which weren't true.

The other thing, which really makes me happy, and for which I am lucky, is that I have family support. My parents have been, for the most part, so good to me, and have done everything they can to help me out.

They still support me and will aid me in my recovery.

The coffee tastes warm, and life is slowly starting to improve.

Chapter 50

ROUTINE

A few days later, I am released from CAMH. My parents pick me up.

We go for lunch at a Japanese restaurant that serves sushi. The food tastes so good. I am so happy to have left the institution.

My parents then drop me off at my condo.

I lie down on the bed and rest for a few hours. I then go downstairs to the grocery store and do some shopping. It is then that I discover the key to improving my life. I really need to be disciplined and be a good person.

I start to do things that make my life so much better. I start practicing the violin every day. I workout in the exercise room in my condo daily. I also write everyday as well as read a lot more.

Happiness, I figure out, really comes from being disciplined. I also ignore the voices and I take my medicine every day.

I visit my parents and my sister and brother-in-law as well as their children every week. Seeing the children grow up, and being able to be a part of their lives, is very rewarding.

I have a routine. I get up early in the morning, around 5 a.m., and go and workout. I then come back, eat breakfast, brush my teeth and then practice my violin. I then do some writing on my blog and then go down to the grocery store, shop and have a cup of coffee.

I also go outside a lot more than before. I walk quite a bit as well. I also follow the news a lot more so I always know what is going on in the world.

I decide not to get a job.

I am on the Ontario Disability Services Plan (ODSP), which helps pay for my medicine. If I get a job, that brings me over $200, I will lose the ODSP. I also think that with my illness, I may be better off not getting a job.

Occasionally, I still hear voices, but I have figured out how to cope with them.

The voices say that I am not working and I am lazy. Instead of reacting to the voices, I simply ignore it. I also realize that I have a mental illness, which means I have a legitimate excuse not to work.

As for delusions, they have gone away.

I am not afraid anymore that the United States government is after me, or that John Lennon is talking to me. I realize that junk food will not make me healthier. I also realize that I am not a rock musician.

Something else I have learned about life is that you should enjoy things that are more mundane and wholesome. Don't lie down and talk to voices all day. Get up, put yourself through a little more pain, and you will feel better.

Don't procrastinate.

When you have something to do, do it right away. When you procrastinate is when you start to feel depressed and stressed out. When you don't procrastinate, you feel much better and you feel a sense of accomplishment, which is very important in life.

As for friends, I don't have very many. However, I see my parents and my sister every week. I realize that having more friends is not the answer to leading a better life. What is best is to be disciplined— if you hang out all day, and accomplish nothing, you feel worse.

I remember my close friend Tim.

We hung out a lot together, but a lot of the time, we didn't feel very good because we were wasting so much time hanging out together.

As for having a wife or a girlfriend, I am fine not having one. I enjoy living in solitude, and as long as I am active, I know the voices will not bother me.

The other thing I do religiously is take my medicine. I don't forget a single day. It is an important part of my treatment, and when I have gone off the medicine, bad things have happened.

As for what I eat, I buy very healthy food. I make sure I eat a lot of fruits and vegetables. A doctor diagnosed me as having Type II diabetes. So, I absolutely need to eat healthily and exercise.

Another thing the voices did was make me feel self-conscious about my looks. I am convinced that people who have anorexia or bulimia may be hearing voices as well, telling them that they don't look good or are not skinny enough.

The way I cope with this is to look at the mirror rarely. The other thing I realize is that it doesn't matter how smart you are, or how good looking you are, what matters the most is that you are a good person.

When you treat other people well, and you avoid getting angry, especially at the voices, you start to feel so much better. Even though I don't believe that Jesus performed miracles, his teaching others to be good people is a very good thing to follow.

Besides all of this, I also want to be an advocate for mental health. CAMH has allowed me to educate others about mental illness. I have written a speech to read to high school students to educate them about mental illness.

I also write about being a good person on a blog. When I write, I can analyze my thoughts and from that, I figure out ways to live a better life. I also listen to CBC radio all day in my condo. CBC has a lot of interesting programs, some on mental illness.

Another thing I have discovered is that I don' t want to be famous — like wanting to be a famous rock star. I just want to be an ordinary person, doing ordinary things every day. Wanting to be a rock star happened because I thought having a good life meant being famous.

As for John Lennon, I still love his music. But all the other stuff that has been written about him, like his battles with the United States government, I learned not to apply that to myself.

I am in no way as famous as John Lennon. And there is no reason for the United States government to be after me. I am not that important. I also like not being that important as well.

I don't fear death either. It may come at any time in one's life. I do take risks, but not like the ones I took before. I like to explore new places in Toronto. Finding new places also gives me a sense of accomplishment.

In the end, if my journey helps even one single person, I am very happy to have shared it. Helping others, in whatever way I can, really makes life worth living, and I am glad to have been of service.

www.ingramcontent.com/pod-product-compliance
Lightning Source LLC
Chambersburg PA
CBHW031153020426
42333CB00013B/643

9781950818068